HALLOWEEN
SPOOKTACULAR

MATTHEW MEAD'S
HALLOWEEN
SPOOKTACULAR

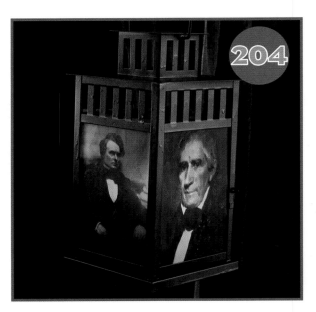

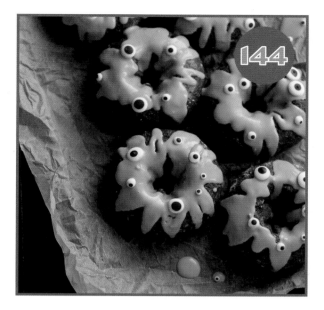

144

154

184

190

220

232

FOUNDER, CREATIVE DIRECTOR, EDITOR IN CHIEF
Matthew Mead
MANAGING EDITOR Jennifer Mead
EXECUTIVE EDITOR Linda Bullock
SENIOR EDITOR Sarah Egge
GRAPHIC DESIGNER
Brian Michael Thomas/Our Hero Productions
STUDIO ASSISTANT/DESIGNER Lisa Bisson

Matthew would like to thank everyone who contributed
their time, talents, and/or invited us into their homes to help
create this special volume, HALLOWEEN SPOOKTACULAR:
Laurie Carey; Michelle and Gary Coffin and their children;
The Courser family of Courser Farm; Lisa Fantasia at Wicked
Unique Cakes and Treats; Joanne Grenon at Grenon Trading
Company; Ryan Linehan at The Kimball-Jenkins Estate;
Bethany Lowe and her team; Marie and Everett Mead; Lisa
Renauld; Sally Robinson at Fancy Flours; Mary and Gordon
Welch; Julie Merberg for her unyielding support; and the
hardworking team at Time Home Entertainment, Inc.

OXMOOR HOUSE

EDITORIAL DIRECTOR Leah McLaughlin
CREATIVE DIRECTOR Felicity Keane
BRAND MANAGER Nina Fleishman
SENIOR EDITORS Andrea C. Kirkland, M.S., R.D.
MANAGING EDITOR Rebecca Benton

MATTHEW MEAD'S HALLOWEEN SPOOKTACULAR
EDITOR Meredith L. Butcher
ART DIRECTOR Claire Cormany
PROJECT EDITOR Emily Chappell
ASSISTANT DESIGNER Allison Sperando Potter
PRODUCTION MANAGER Theresa Beste-Farley

PUBLISHER Jim Childs
VICE PRESIDENT, BRAND & DIGITAL STRATEGY
Steven Sandonato
EXECUTIVE DIRECTOR, MARKETING SERVICES
Carol Pittard
EXECUTIVE DIRECTOR, RETAIL & SPECIAL SALES
Tom Mifsud
**DIRECTOR, BOOKAZINE DEVELOPMENT &
MARKETING** Laura Adam
EXECUTIVE PUBLISHING DIRECTOR Joy Butts
EDITORIAL DIRECTOR Stephen Koepp
ASSOCIATE PUBLISHING DIRECTOR Megan Pearlman
FINANCE DIRECTOR Glenn Buonocore
ASSOCIATE GENERAL COUNSEL Helen Wan

SPECIAL THANKS Katherine Barnet, Jeremy Biloon, Susan
Chodakiewicz, Rose Cirrincione, Jacqueline Fitzgerald,
Christine Font, Jenna Goldberg, Hillary Hirsch, David Kahn,
Mona Li, Amy Mangus, Nina Mistry, Dave Rozzelle, Ricardo
Santiago, Adriana Tierno, Vanessa Wu

ISBN 10: 0-8487-3455-6
ISBN 13: 978-0-8487-3455-8

We welcome your comments and suggestions about Time
Home Entertainment Books. Please write to us at: Time
Home Entertainment Books, Attention: Book Editors, P.O.
Box 11016, Des Moines, IA 50336-1016

If you would like to order any of our hardcover Collector's
Edition books, please call us at 1-800-327-6388, Monday
through Friday, 7 a.m. to 8 p.m., or Saturday, 7 a.m. to 6 p.m.,
Central Time.

With any craft project, check product labels to make sure that the materials you use are safe and
nontoxic. The instructions in this book are intended to be followed with adult supervision.

NOTE: Neither the publisher nor the author is responsible for your specific health or allergy needs that
may require medical supervision, or for any adverse reactions to the recipes contained in this book.

This year I want you to view my new Halloween Spooktacular book like the Sears Christmas Wish Book of the past. Its 256 pages are meant to conjure the kind of seasonally inspired ponderings that the Wish Book did when I sat cross-legged and held it in my lap each year. Only this time, the Spooktacular book fosters dreams of Halloween crafting, decorating, gathering, and celebrating.

All year long I've worked to fill the book with pages and pages of step-by-step projects, hundreds of fun ideas, and loads of budget-conscious ways to "haunt" your house with what you already have on hand. My hope is that you (and your children) will leaf through it over and over. They may nudge you to throw a costume party, decorate the front porch, or have friends over to decorate donuts. I hope you will be urged to visit the local pumpkin patch and pick the perfect pumpkin for carving, or take the time to dress up your dog in the sweetest Halloween costume you can cobble together.

Like the festive ideas offered in the Sears Wish Book, my Spooktacular book includes ways to dress up every room in your home, including the entryway, the living room, the dining room, and even the mantel. I've added parties for folks of all ages, for families, for kids, and for couples looking to engage the season—and some nostalgia. The book is colorful and offers simple-to-replicate ideas, so that you can streamline the preparation and have more time to gather the family and instill some new traditions.

Just like my mother did with the Wish Book, you can keep the Spooktacular book out all season long, until the pages get dog-eared from use. Leave it on the coffee table with a bowl of candy corn, so everyone can dream up Halloween visions. I'll be taking ideas from the pages to use at my own house, stringing orange ball lights in the front tree and hanging orange-and-black paper medallions like bunting from the edge of my porch roof. I hope you find plenty of simple ideas to give your home a very special Halloween feel.

Happy Halloween to each and every one of you.

TRADE SECRETS

In the days leading up to Halloween, it is easy to scare up ideas if you're prepared. Here is our "go-to" kit for all of your decorating ideas … even the last minute ones.

BITS AND PIECES

Make space in your craft room to work, and bring
in some festive colors to put you in the mood.
Matthew transformed an old artist's box with
black paint and labels he made (you can make
similar ones using Photoshop®). Simply découpage
the label onto the box using Mod Podge®, and fill
the inside with all of your supplies.

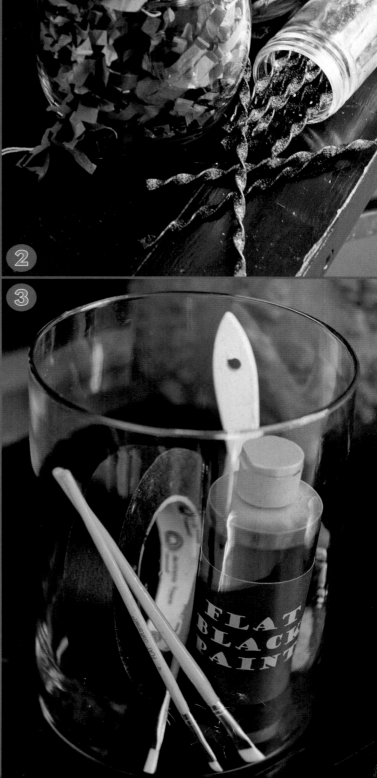

TOOLS OF THE TRADE

Matthew is always up on a ladder hanging something, so a faux mini pumpkin studded with pushpins (OPPOSITE) is a great tool to perch on the top rung—if the pumpkin falls, the tacks won't scatter and a miniature pumpkin rolling along the floor offers up a bit of a haunted vibe. When decorating for holidays it is always helpful to keep everything at the ready for any whimsical décor urge: **1.** An orange bowl sets off black plastic spiders, making them easy for the eyes to find when looking for spooky embellishments. **2.** Supplies like paper garland, spiders, and Halloween icicles—all from BethanyLowe.com—look great in jars. We added a grommet to the top of a storage jar to easily dispense vintage-inspired tissue garland. **3.** You will need black flat paint for many of the projects in this issue; Matthew always keeps it close at hand with an assortment of brushes. Corral everything, including some black tape, in an old jar or glass for easy organization.

ORDER IN THE COURT

Organize your decorating supplies: **1.** Screw-top storage jars are great for holding spiders, bugs, and glow-in-thedark stars. **2.** Outfit the inside of the art box with a cork tile. Use it to organize small amounts of items like plastic rodents, scissors for cutting, and extra Zots® for holding almost everything in place. **3.** The base of an old metal fondue pot is perfect for dispensing the spider webbing needed to add fear factor to porches and doorways. **4.** We created specialty labels using Photoshop® and printed them for use on boxes, ribbon spools, and jars.

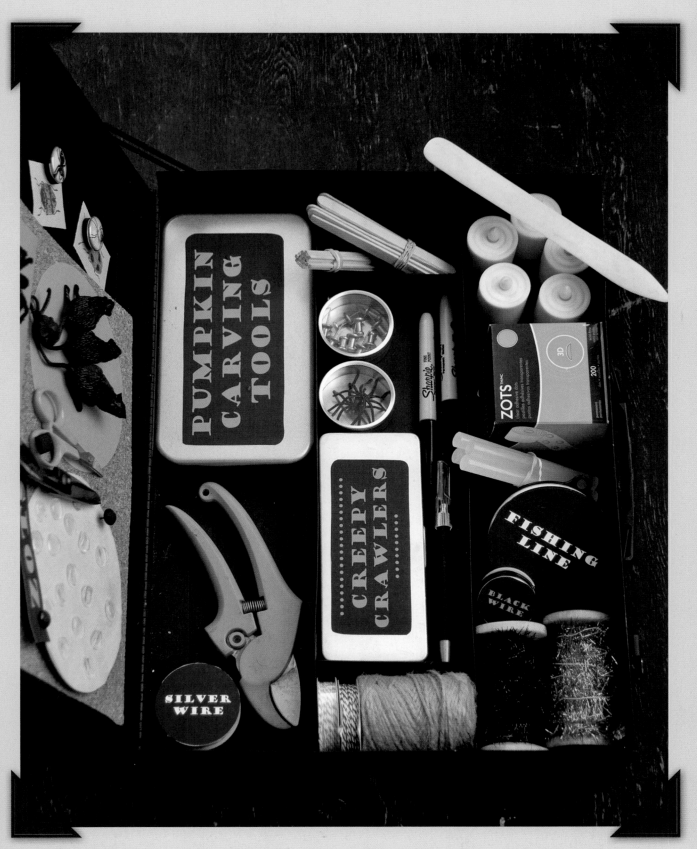

ESSENTIALS

Fill a supply case with the following necessities: pumpkin carving tools; wooden picks and popsicle sticks to make into drink and cupcake embellishments; a bone folder for paper projects; fuss-free battery-operated votive candles; sturdy metal pushpins for hanging decorations; extra plastic spiders, bugs, and snakes; black Sharpie® markers; an X-Acto™ knife, scissors, and wire cutters; Zots®; hot glue sticks; and fishing line, wire, tinsel, and twine.

PEST CONTROL

Nothing makes skin crawl like the sight of insects taking over every corner of a house. But when the bugs are plastic and occur only at Halloween, collective sighs of relief make way for giggles of delight. We embraced the updated tradition of gathering neighborhood trick-or-treaters for a lively porch party—where revellers seek out treats and mingle with a

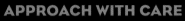

APPROACH WITH CARE

A bounty of orange and white pumpkins line the steps to the porch where an errant ghost greets trick-or-treaters. Three-dimensional Mylar spider stickers add a creepy-crawly note to each pumpkin, signalling the theme.

CREEPY CRAWLIES

A vintage globe—painted black and decorated with glow-in-the-dark beetle stickers—rests atop a stack of books about insects. Small ribbon-wrapped votives cast a warm glow on the vignette, and a humble plastic spider becomes fancy when placed in a bejewelled picture frame.

THE INSECT BOOK — HOWARD

DOUBLEDAY PAGE & CO.

CAUGHT IN A WEB

Rest a wire spider's web in the crook of a tree and find small webs in the jewelry supply aisle of a craft store to fashion a spooky garland. String beads and the webs with monofilament wire and use them to festoon Halloween trees or porch railings.

E ntomologists study them. Arachnophobes recoil at the eight-legged variety. Little children—young and unaffected enough to still be enamored with them—scoop bugs out from the dirt and bottle them up in clear glass jars, marvelling at their hairy bodies, pointy feelers, and wiggly legs. And, yet, for the vast majority of us, insects are feared, cursed, swatted away, or squished in our haste to escape their seemingly lightning fast movements and hair-raising peskiness. But when Halloween rolls around, insects somehow find a place among us where they are actually invited in, given a temporary invitation to hang around and creep us out—with one important condition: they can't actually be real. We rounded up a collection of faux flies, roaches, and spiders and used them to inspire a Halloween porch party whose focus is on fun décor and fuss-free food. Trick-or-treating parties are the perfect alternative to sending little ones out house-to-house in search of their candy, and by keeping the food simple, more time can be spent on setting the scene. Invite your neighbors and their children over to gather on your porch for candy bags, sweet treats you can find at your local grocery store, and use a few bags of multi-legged, plastic "friends" ahead of time to create fanciful (but hair-raising!) Halloween crafts that are sure to delight little ones—while creeping out those who have long lost their affection for the tiny space invaders known simply as *bugs*.

ENTER IF YOU DARE
The simple act of opening the door elicits shivers as a foreboding wreath, wrapped in cobwebs, offers a sticky surprise for guests as they arrive at the porch party. Find the how-to directions on page 32.

BUG INFESTATION

The bugs have landed: **1.** A plastic spider adorns the cover of an old photo album. **2.** A bug-infested pumpkin tops a large urn—placed strategically in the pathway for guests to skirt around as they make their way to the porch. **3.** Use an old photo frame to display a faux black widow spider and hang it on a door. **4.** Fill an urn with black curly willow and place it in the center of the table.

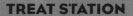

TREAT STATION
A metal flea market
factory table bears
a Halloween topiary,
Jack-Be-Little pumpkins,
and an assortment of
Halloween treats—such
as cream-filled horns,
cookies, and donuts—
and is one of the treat
zones on the porch.

MARCHING TWO BY TWO

Three-dimensional spider stickers from Michaels creep along the surface of each pumpkin on the steps leading up to the porch. Their crinkly Mylar bodies and legs make them rustle in the wind—giving the illusion that they are alive and moving. Look for a mixture of colors and sizes at local farm stands and grocery stores.

"By keeping the treats simple you can focus on the fun stuff: the Halloween decorations and your costume!"
—Matthew

STICKY SWEET

For those whom just the thought of baking and cooking for a party sends shivers up their spines, a trip to the local grocery store will supply all that is needed to satisfy the sweet tooth of any trick-or-treater. Bring home a ready-baked pumpkin pie (ABOVE) and crown it with a ring of black licorice drops. To up the "ick" factor, dab the ends of hors d'oeuvres picks with hot glue and stick them into the underside of small plastic bugs; insert the bug picks into the pie. Jelly-filled donuts and chocolate-covered cookies fill a nearby tray (LEFT), and the chocolate cookie coating mimics a spider's web. Use more of the bug picks to poke into the sweet treats. With all of the sugar on hand for Halloween, serve tall glasses of cold milk (OPPOSITE) to temper some of the sweetness. Here, glass tumblers are wrapped with ribbon and embellished with metal Halloween buttons (find directions on page 36). Secure the ends of the ribbon to the glasses using Zots™. For a "suspicious" beverage alternative, fill a glass bottle with apple juice—darkened with black food coloring. Find the drink label template on page 240.

Bug
juice

Squashed from bugs
that live on a
SPRUCE
filtered and sieved
to make a
JUICE.

BUZZ-WORTHY SNACKS

No bug swatter is needed to shoo the flies away from these Boston-cream cookies. Sturdy toothpicks, painted black, are inserted into the bottom of large plastic flies and poked into the jimmy-coated cookies.

FRIGHT

DELIGHT

&

be SCARY

GRAB BAG
Halloween treat bags from the craft store are filled
with an assortment of candy and await little guests.
Punch holes in the top of each bag and thread black
and white baker's twine through each hole to secure.

LIGHT BRIGHT
Small, inexpensive votives—
embellished with ribbon—add
flickering light to the party décor.
Buy in bulk and use battery-
operated candles for fuss-free
illumination. All project directions
begin on page 28.

BUG'S NEST

Guests are sure to recoil in fear as they come upon hanging bug sacs—seemingly ready to burst open, allowing their creepy contents to scatter and escape. Follow the directions on page 31 to make your own.

HOW TO: SPIDER PUMPKIN

WHAT YOU'LL NEED

- Large pumpkin(s)
- Circle template (we used a Fiskars® circle punch)
- Permanent marker
- Pumpkin carving tools
- Black, plastic insects
- Push pins (we used black ball-topped pins)
- Glass votive
- Battery-operated candle

1. Use the pumpkin carving tools to clean out and prepare your pumpkin for carving. Remove all of the pulp and seeds and scrape the inner surface clean. Using a marker, trace around the circle template until you have the desired number of circles all around the pumpkin. Cut out the circles using a small carving tool, and scrape the inner part of each round opening lightly until clean and smooth.

2. Poke a push pin through each plastic bug and insert the bug firmly into the center of each round opening in the pumpkin. Insert two bugs into several of the holes and secure additional bugs into the top of the pumpkin.

3. Place a battery-operated candle into a votive and set it inside the pumpkin. Place your lit pumpkin atop a cake stand, urn, or stack of books for dramatic effect. Nestle a faux insect into several votives and arrange alongside the pumpkin to illuminate the scene.

"I buy bags of plastic bugs each Halloween for my craft projects. You can never have too many!"
—Matthew

HOW TO: BUG TREE

- ❍ Grapevine cone (from a craft store or florist's shop)
- ❍ White acrylic paint
- ❍ Paint brush
- ❍ One package of faux spider webbing
- ❍ Black, plastic insects
- ❍ Hot-glue gun and glue sticks
- ❍ Black urn or pot

1. Use a dry paint brush to apply a thin coat of white paint to the grapevine cone, giving it a white-washed effect; let dry.

2. Gently pull apart the faux webbing and wrap it around the cone. The rough surface of the cone will easily hold the webbing in place.

3. Use a hot glue gun to adhere plastic insects to the surface of the cone, placing the insects as though they are climbing up the tree. Set the bug tree atop a pot or urn and use as a centerpiece (see photo, page 20). Make several for use as mantel décor indoors or to line the length of a large table.

HOW TO: BUG'S NEST

WHAT YOU'LL NEED

- ❍ Wire, grapevine, or Styrofoam® ball
- ❍ One package of faux spider webbing
- ❍ 16-guage floral wire
- ❍ Wire cutter
- ❍ Needle-nose pliers
- ❍ Hot glue gun and glue sticks
- ❍ Black, plastic winged insects

1. Take a length of floral wire and wrap it around the ball or sphere several times. Before snipping with the wire cutter, continue to roll out the wire to a length of approximately 15-inches more and make the cut. This will form the long, slender neck of the bug's nest.

2. Gently pull apart the faux webbing and begin wrapping it around the ball and hanging length of wire. Use dabs of hot glue to secure the web in place.

3. Use the hot glue gun to adhere plastic insects to the surface of the sphere and up the length of the hanging wire. For that "about-to-hatch" effect, tuck some of the plastic flies behind the webbing in spots. Make several bugs' nests and hang along the eaves of the porch, from branches or along the porch railing. To hang, use needle-nose pliers to curl the end of the vertical length of wire and hook the curled end onto a nail or cup hook.

HOW TO:
SPIDER WREATH

WHAT YOU'LL NEED

- One 12 to 14-inch grapevine wreath
- One package of faux spider webbing
- Silver glitter spray paint (find at a craft store)
- Hot glue gun and glue sticks
- 12 plastic spiders

1. Using newspaper or craft paper as your work surface, apply one coat of glitter spray paint (using manufacturer's directions) evenly to both sides of a grapevine wreath—allowing each side to dry thoroughly between paint applications.

2. Stretch out the sheets of faux webbing and begin wrapping it around the surface of the wreath. Pull the webbing apart from the inner edges of the wreath so it resembles a spun web.

3. Use a hot glue gun to attach plastic spiders to the front of the wreath. Hang from a wreath hanger or doorknob (OPPOSITE) to provide guests with a sticky greeting.

HOW TO: SPIDER CANDLE HOLDERS

WHAT YOU'LL NEED

- ❍ Wired organdy ribbon (look for bug-themed ribbon in the Halloween section of the craft store)
- ❍ Small glass votives
- ❍ Tea lights or small battery-operated candles
- ❍ Scissors
- ❍ Double-stick tape or Zots®

1. Assemble the desired number of votives and enough ribbon, tea lights, and tape to complete the project. Arrange a cluster of votives on a table or line them up along the porch rail.

2. To determine the length of ribbon needed for each votive, unspool the ribbon and wrap it around the circumference of the votive; use scissors to cut the required length.

3. Secure each end of the ribbon to the glass using double-stick tape or Zots®. Insert a tea light or battery-operated candle into each votive. (Note: do not leave lit candles unattended or within reach of children.)

HOW TO: BUG TOOTHPICKS

WHAT YOU'LL NEED

- Toothpicks (we used hors d'oeuvre picks)
- Black acrylic paint
- Small paint brush
- Plastic flies and spiders
- Block of floral foam
- Hot glue gun

1. Place each plastic insect on its back. Poke a small hole into the belly of each bug using a toothpick. Remove the toothpick and squeeze a small dab of hot glue into the hole.

2. Press the toothpick back firmly into the hole in each bug and let set for 60 seconds.

3. Invert each insect pick and poke it into the foam block. Using a paintbrush, apply a coat of black paint to each toothpick and let dry. Use the bug picks to embellish desserts and treats (see photo, page 22).

HOW TO: CANDY HOLDERS

WHAT YOU'LL NEED

- ❍ Glass votives, jelly jars, and drinking glasses
- ❍ Wired ribbon or decorative binding tape
- ❍ Brown scrapbook paper
- ❍ Pencil
- ❍ Scissors
- ❍ Hot glue gun
- ❍ Zots®
- ❍ Assorted Halloween candy
- ❍ Halloween-themed metal buttons (we purchased ours at Etsy.com/Shop/Funcreations5)

1. Gather a selection of black and white ribbon and use Halloween buttons or stickers to dress up the covers for each candy cup and drinking glass.

2. Invert each jelly jar or votive onto a 12x12-inch piece of brown scrapbook paper. Using a pencil, trace around the rim of the votives. Set the glass aside and cut out a circle for use as a topper for each votive candy holder—perfect for "keeping the bugs out"—and use hot glue to secure one metal button to the top of every scrapbook-paper circle. Wrap ribbon or binding tape around each votive and drinking glass and secure the ends of the ribbon to the glass using Zots®. Fill the votives with Halloween candies (OPPOSITE) and top them with the embellished paper circles. Glue metal buttons to the ribbon-wrapped drinking glasses and fill with milk, juice, or "potion" (see photo, page 23).

It's easy to change the look of glass votives when you use a removable Zot® the secure the ribbon on.

1

2

CREATURES FROM THE DEEP

The thought of an elusive sea creature emerging from the darkest depths is enough to send chills rippling up and down spines. Sieze these spooky images for quick decorations. Anyone can put a face on a pumpkin—you'll attract more oohs and aahs with face-sucking jellyfish and spear-throwing tritons.

EERIE AND EASY

Not only are these silhouettes unique and clever pumpkin decorations—they're a cinch to do! Simply cut the shapes from black construction or scrapbook paper, then pin them in place. A snaky sea serpent twines menacingly (OPPOSITE). You don't have to live near a beach to nestle a jack featuring a pinching fish into an empty planter or fountain (ABOVE). Use the dangling tentacles on a horrifying jellyfish to garner attention (RIGHT).

OCEAN LORE

In this scene, Triton guards his mermaid with a threatening looking trident. In addition to real creatures, you can use the imaginative fodder of spooky sea stories—from mythology to *Moby Dick* to *Jaws*—to inspire your choice of decorative motifs.

OCTO-FUN
The arms of this octopus seem to reach out to grab passers-by. Add to the sticky trap by stuffing cooked spaghetti noodles into the pumpkin's cavity and letting them drape out of the opening.

HORSE TALES

A friendlier image of a sea horse is featured on this pumpkin. Children will have fun helping you pick the watery motifs, and you can let them cut out the simpler shapes themselves.

BY THE TAIL

A novel pumpkin decoration, this whale is perfect for an elongated gourd tipped over, or for one that sits naturally on its side. You could add smaller whales to the other side to create a circling pod, or simply let this one call to mind all the great whale tales you've heard.

HOW TO: SILHOUETTES

WHAT YOU'LL NEED

- Sea creature motifs starting on page 241 or from HolidayWithMatthewMead.com
- Pencil
- Cutting mat
- Xcto® knife
- Small scissors
- Black scrapbook paper
- Stickpins with black heads

1. Trace the sea creature's outline onto the black paper using a pencil. Cut out the images using an Xacto knife to get into the tiny openings. These silhouettes are captivating because they are so detailed, so all the tedious nooks and crannies help with the scare-factor.

2. For the easier shapes and smooth edges, use small scissors. Children can help out, or let them make their own imaginative shapes. Sharks, crabs, and stingrays are still creepy but easier to cut out.

3. Position the silhouette on the pumpkin and use stickpins to hold it in place. When the season is over, remove the pins and save the silhouette for next year.

Scrapbook paper has a nice weight for these projects; construction paper can be too flimsy and card stock is too rigid.

1

2

HAUNTING YOUR HOUSE

Step inside the home of Matthew and Jenny Mead, where they've made decorating their hallowed halls a ghostly affair with some not-so-daunting ideas straight from their bag of stylists' tricks.

WHITE AS A SHEET

Plain cotton sheets, draped over furniture, announce the spirited theme in the Meads' living room. Orange pumpkins and black accents round out the traditional palette, and set the tone that these are friendly ghosts.

OUT OF THE DARK
A photocopied or scanned image of a black cat is slipped inside a clear glass lamp base. Topped with a polka-dotted orange shade, it is a simple way to bring a Halloween vibe to any room. Find the lamp and shade directions on page 56.

THRILLS AND CHILLS

Wooden plaques (LEFT) or pieces of slate from the craft store can be painted with chalkboard paint and scribbled with sayings, dates, and iconic images—perfect for a spooky wall-art treatment or lined up on mounted shelves. Ghosts large and small dictate the room's décor (RIGHT). Whether they are friendly or menacing depends largely on the shape and placement of their eyes.

Matthew Mead practices what he preaches—especially when it comes to decorating his own home—and his motto centers on using what you already have. "I love to poke through my craft supplies, unearth items in the basement, and rediscover cast-off pieces in the attic," says Matthew. "And because my home is always in design transition, I like to repurpose items as something new and different."

With that in mind, an entry hall coat rack becomes a stylish standing spectre, a sofa morphs into a beckoning ghost, and a built-in glass-fronted cupboard masquerades as a window from which ghostly apparitions peer out. And because his wife, Jenny, shares his penchant for inspired Halloween décor, she helps out by creating projects like the collection of chalk drawings found throughout the main floor. A bit of a technological whiz, Jenny also uses her computer to design and print decorative images to use on lamps and around candleholders. Enlisting family and friends to help with the decorating only adds to the fun: "We all enjoy using our Halloween craft kit (see page TK) to create and embellish pumpkins, lampshades, and framed prints that can adorn the walls," says Matthew. "Honestly, Halloween decorating doesn't have to involve a visit to a department store to achieve a clever design scheme. By using my decorating tricks, you can spend those savings on treats!"

GHOST BUSTERS

The Meads dressed up as ghosts, took photographs, and used an online photo program to resize the photos. After printing them at a copy center, they used double-stick tape to apply the images to the glass panes of a cupboard.

EERIE ETCHINGS

Jenny has a love of fonts and a knack for drawing. She combined those interests to create a gallery of chalkboard art to line the shelves of the living room. Follow the directions on page 54 to make your own.

FELINE FLAIR

A black velvet pumpkin from Halloween guru Bethany Lowe is given cat features with the addition of some eyes, whiskers, and a button nose. A steady hand and some white paint is all you need to create this seasonal statement. The addition of a patterned pillow, in a cheery orange, brings color and interest to the sofa.

GHOSTLY GOURDS
A cauldron of faux white gourds from years past are reborn with a mix of painted eye designs—each one with its very own personality.

HOW TO: CHALK PLAQUES

WHAT YOU'LL NEED

- ❍ Wooden plaques from the craft store
- ❍ Black chalkboard paint
- ❍ Paint brush
- ❍ Small sanding block
- ❍ Chalk
- ❍ Sample fonts printed from your computer

1. Apply a coat of chalkboard paint to the wooden plaques. Let dry according to manufacturer's instructions and give the plaques a light sanding before applying a second coat.

2. Print off your desired font (or design your own) and use as a guide to create your own chalkboard design. Use white chalk to outline and fill in the image or letters. If you prefer a more muted, chalky background, follow the directions on the paint can to season the painted plaque before applying the chalk design. This extra step also makes it easier to erase if you wish to switch out the designs often. Paint a number of plaques using different designs and arrange them on shelves (OPPOSITE) for an instant gallery effect.

Check out Dover copyright-free books for Halloween images to inspire your chalkboard designs.

SPELLS & POTIONS

chills

1892

HOW TO: POLKA-DOT LAMP

WHAT YOU'LL NEED

- Glass lamp base (with a removable top or open bottom)
- Colorful shade
- Black scrapbook paper
- Fiskars® circle punch
- Double-sided tape
- Black cat print (template at HolidayWithMatthewMead.com)

1. Scan or photocopy the cat image and slip it inside the glass lamp base. Punch out paper polka dots using the circle punch.

2. Secure the polka dots to the surface of the shade using double-sided tape. Apply the polka dots in a random fashion, leaving space between each circle.

> "My goal each season is to give familiar ideas a fresh spin. Halloween decorating should be fun!"
> —Matthew

HOW TO: GHOSTLY COAT RACK

- Coat rack (choose a sturdy one with a stable base)
- Hollowed out faux pumpkin
- White sheet
- Black adhesive-backed felt
- Scissors

1. Place the hollowed out faux pumpkin over the top of the coat rack.

2. Drape the sheet over the coat rack to determine where the face of the ghost will be. Use scissors to cut out eye shapes from the black felt and remove the paper backing to reveal the sticky underside. Adhere the eyes onto the sheet, situating them over the "face" of the ghost.

3. Adjust the pumpkin and sheet so that the head is secure and the eyes are facing forward. Place the coat rack in a location where it will not be an obstacle to passers-by.

HOW TO: BLACK CAT CUSHION

WHAT YOU'LL NEED

○ Black velvet or fabric pumpkin
○ Black felt
○ Scissors
○ White acrylic paint
○ Small artist's paint brush
○ Fabric glue
○ Large button
○ Hot glue gun and glue

1. Gather what you will need to make this charming cat cushion. Use scissors to cut out two black felt cat ears; set aside.

2. Use white paint to create two identical cat eyes, using our photo as a guide. Leave the center unpainted (SEE BELOW) to mimic the pupil of each eye. Once the paint is dry, use hot glue to attach the cat's button nose and apply several dabs of fabric (or hot) glue to the bottom edge of each ear and secure in place.

HOW TO: GHOSTLY GOURDS

WHAT YOU'LL NEED

- ○ Small white gourds (real or faux)
- ○ Black permanent marker
- ○ Black acrylic paint
- ○ Small paint brush

1. Mini white faux gourds come to life with the simple addition of a pair of painted, black eyes. Use a permanent marker to outline the eye shapes, making some appear friendly; others spooky.

2. Use black acrylic paint to fill in the eye shapes. A small artist's brush will work best to create a neat silhouette. By using faux gourds, the adorable little ghosts will last from year to year.

"Our 'frightfully uncommon' ideas will leave guests thinking you have expensive designer ghosts living with you."
—Matthew

HOW TO: HAUNTED HANGOUT

- Sofa or chair
- Faux pumpkin
- Zots®
- Black adhesive-backed felt
- White marking pencil
- Scissors
- Large white sheet
- Pencil

1. Trace out two corresponding eye shapes onto the black felt using the white marking pencil. Cut out the shapes and set aside.

2. Apply 4-6 Zots® to the bottom of the pumpkin and secure it to the top edge of the sofa. Situate the pumpkin onto the top corner of the sofa or chair. Drape the white sheet over the seat and pumpkin, and tuck in the sheet to the seat frame. Use a pencil to lightly mark where the eyes should be placed.

3. Pull the sheet down off the pumpkin and remove the paper backing of the felt eyes to reveal the sticky side. Using the pencil markings as a guide, stick the eyes onto the sheet, pressing to secure.

4. Pull the sheet back up over the pumpkin and adjust it down over the back of the seat. Make necessary adjustments to the sheet to ensure the eyes are situated correctly within the face of the pumpkin.

LIGHTS IN THE NIGHT

The Courser family lights hundreds of jack-o'-lanterns on its Warner, New Hampshire, farm in the nights before Halloween. It's a community event that draws people from far and wide to carve pumpkins, and then return for the glowing show. When you carve this many pumpkins, you learn a few tricks, which Rebecca Courser is happy to share. Read on for some of the cutting ins and outs of this fun seasonal activity.

FACE TIME

People pack picnics to eat off hay bales (ABOVE, LEFT) while they wait for the jacks to be lit. You can carve as many pumpkins as you wish (ABOVE, RIGHT). Rebecca Courser, whose family started this tradition 16 years ago, says it takes lots of help to ignite all the candles (OPPOSITE). This year, the carving event will be Sunday, October 27 from 12 to 4 p.m. The evening glow will be held every night from then through the 31st.

Turn the bend and shine your headlights down Schoodac Road. It's a crisp evening before Halloween, and you've heard there's a sight to see at Courser Farm. Ahead of you, flickering across the rolling fields that fan down the valley toward the white farmhouse and back up again, is the glow of hundreds of carved pumpkins. Like an army of large fireflies, they burn orange and gold in staggered rows. You want to stop and get a closer look, so you park along the berm and walk the acres, pausing to admire the crooked smiles and warm hearts, the abstract patterns and the evil grins. Each pumpkin is different, but they form a whole—an undulating carpet of jack-o'-lanterns.

Now in its 16th year, this spectacle is the result of the hard work of generations of Coursers. Rebecca lives in the farmhouse with her husband, daughter, and grandchildren. Her brothers, Gerald and Tim, run the farm. Everyone lives close and puts in countless hours on the event. The jack-o'-lanterns, which number as many as 1,200, are good uses for what doesn't sell off their patch. "These are the second-grade pumpkins," Rebecca says. "They might have a weak stem or a soft spot or they aren't totally orange." The family scoops out the seeds, then people are invited to carve on the Sunday afternoon before Halloween.

SUMMIT OF SQUASH
The jack-o'-lanterns line the road and snake off
into the fields in walkable rows. The family tries to
elevate as many as possible on fence posts, hay
bales, and wagons to create interesting displays.

CARVING TECHNIQUES

"The cutting is different every year," Rebecca says, depending on whether the squashes are wet (it's easier) or dry (a little tougher). **1.** A small paring knife is her tool of choice. **2.** All the pumpkin innards are fed to the cattle. "They love it," she says. **3.** "Orange-handled carving kits are great tools," Rebecca says. But people bring all kinds of things (often cordless drills and bits) for specialty cuts. **4.** Some people follow a pattern, other's sketch it out or freehand it. "I'm a square and triangle cutter," she says.

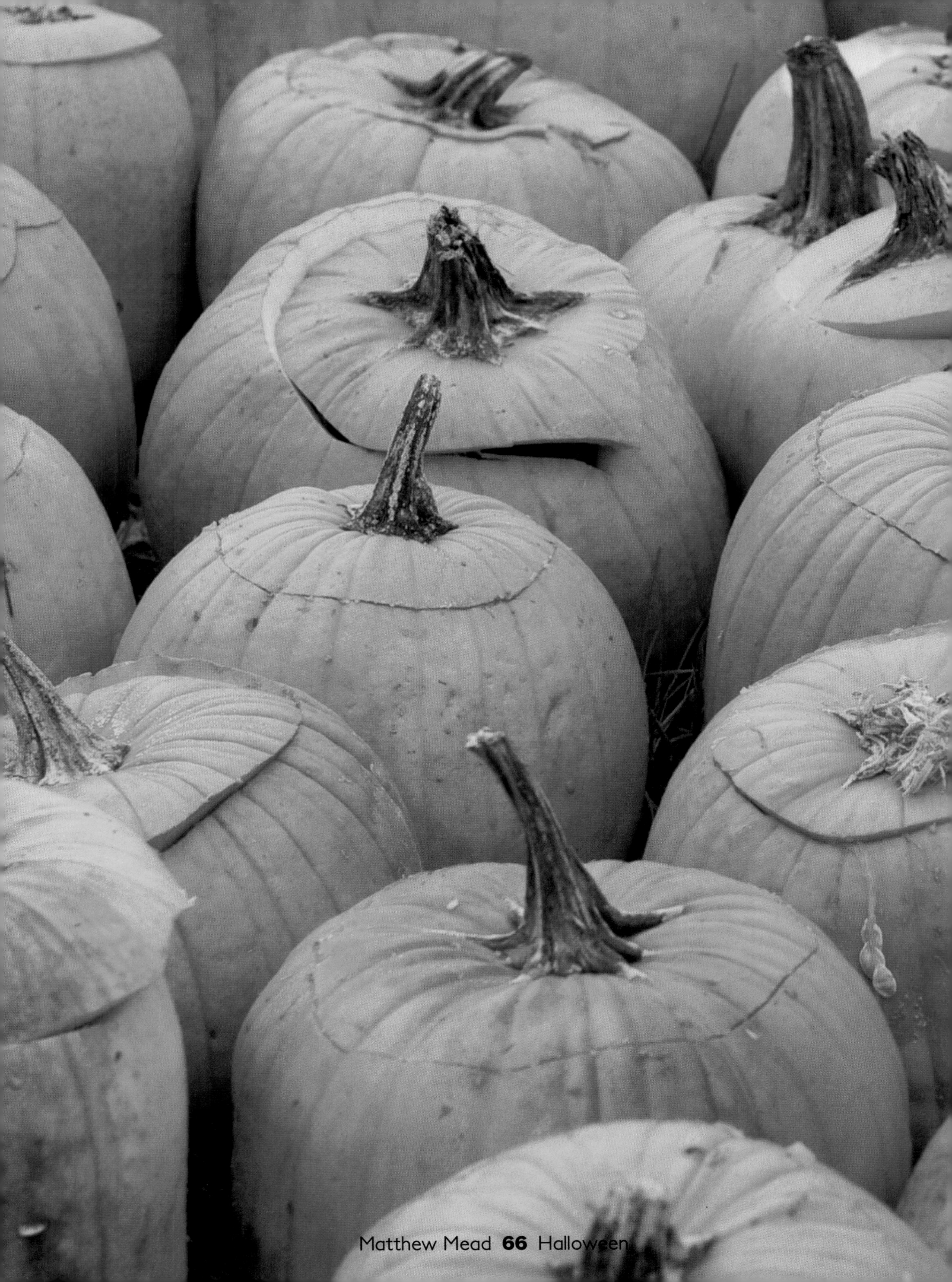

The Coursers grow many varieties on about seven acres to get pumpkins of different shapes, sizes, and colors. Amish Pie and Cinderella are some of their stand-bys.

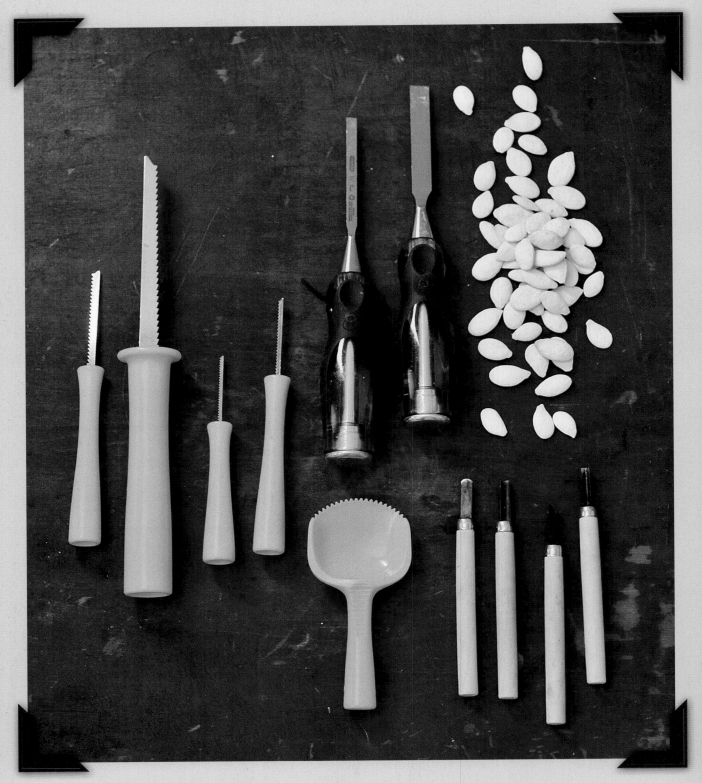

TOOLS OF THE TRADE

Although you can carve a fine pumpkin using a soup spoon and a steak knife, you'll have an easier and more creative time with better tools—and you'll be able to accomplish intricate features (OPPOSITE). Orange-handled pumpkin-carving knives, scoops, and chisels (ABOVE) are easiest to use. Rebecca loves the scoop for hollowing out squash innards. "It's squat and sturdy and lets you scrape the sides," she says. Look for them at crafts stores, home centers, and in the seasonal aisles of retailers like Wal-Mart and Target. The metal- and wood-handled blades are woodcarving tools from a crafts or hobby store. They have sharply honed edges that let you make small, precise cuts, but you have to use them with care. They're also good for etching designs, where you carve away the tough outer skin and whittle the soft flesh, like the gap-toothed jack (OPPOSITE, BOTTOM RIGHT CORNER).

SMILEY FACE

A happy jack sits on a rock wall on the Courser farm. "We don't make it a scary event," Rebecca says. The family puts together a few scarecrows ("When we have time"), but avoid anything frightening. "We don't want to scare little kids," she says. "It's not like a haunted house feeling at all."

HOW TO: CANDLELIGHTS

WHAT YOU'LL NEED

- ○ Acrylic votive candleholder
- ○ Small pebbles
- ○ Battery-operated tea light candles
- ○ Plastic wrap

1. The Courser family sets 1-inch votive candles, which they buy by the case, in plastic drinking cups in their jack-o'-lanterns. But that requires nightly relighting. For a less-messy and weatherproof option, fill a candleholder with a ½-inch layer of small pebbles. This will elevate the candle, so the glow shines more directly out the carved openings.

2. Tuck in the battery-operated light.

3. Seal the top of the candleholder tightly with plastic wrap to keep out moisture from rain or dew.

4. You can keep the light turned on (LED lights can last up to 60 hours) or turn it off each night.

The firelight inside pumpkin lanterns is meant to scare away ghosts and witches on Halloween. Long ago, people tried the same trick using carved turnips, potatoes, and beets.

1

2

FAMILY FUN
Most years, guests (above) enjoy idyllic weather in middle New Hampshire. But Rebecca and the family has come to expect it all—rain or shine or even the odd hurricane—and the jack-o'-lanterns still get lit. "One year, we got 14 inches of snow. We shoveled off the pumpkins, set them on top of the snow, and lit them again," she says.

PETER, PETER PUMPKIN EATER

This clever display shows a large jack-o'-lantern "eating" a smaller one. To set this up, the large gourd had a big chunk cut out where the mouth would be, and it was elevated slightly on a brick. Then the smaller jack was tucked up to it.

HOW TO: PUMPKIN PECAN CAKE

- ❍ 1½ cups all-purpose flour
- ❍ ½ cup white whole-wheat flour
- ❍ 2 tablespoons ground flax
- ❍ ½ cup finely chopped toasted pecans
- ❍ 2 teaspoons baking soda
- ❍ ½ teaspoon salt
- ❍ 2 teaspoons ground cinnamon
- ❍ ½ teaspoon ground ginger
- ❍ ¼ teaspoon ground nutmeg
- ❍ ¼ teaspoon ground cloves
- ❍ ¼ teaspoon ground allspice
- ❍ 4 large eggs
- ❍ 1⅓ cups granulated sugar
- ❍ ⅓ cup vegetable oil
- ❍ ½ cup unsweetened applesauce
- ❍ 1 15-ounce can pumpkin puree
- ❍ 2 teaspoons vanilla extract

Preheat oven to 350°.

1. Lightly spray a large Bundt pan with cooking spray; set aside.

2. In a large bowl, whisk together flours, flax, pecans, baking soda, salt, cinnamon, ginger, nutmeg, cloves, and allspice. Set aside.

3. Using an electric stand mixer or hand-mixer on medium speed, beat eggs thoroughly. Add sugar and beat until pale yellow, light, and fluffy, about 3 to 4 minutes. Gradually add oil, applesauce, pumpkin, and vanilla, beating well after each addition.

4. With the mixer on low speed, blend in flour mixture several spoonfuls at a time, beating only until flour is moistened. To avoid over-mixing, stop the mixer early and finish blending the ingredients by hand with a spoon.

5. Pour batter into prepared pan and bake for 45 minutes. Remove from oven and cool for 45 minutes in the pan. Loosen edge, invert cake onto cooling rack; cool thoroughly.

HOW TO:
PUMPKIN MOLASSES COOKIES

WHAT YOU'LL NEED

- 1½ tablespoons pumpkin pie spice
- ¼ cup granulated sugar
- 2⅓ cups all-purpose flour
- 2 teaspoons baking soda
- ½ teaspoon baking powder
- 2 teaspoons cinnamon
- 1½ teaspoons ground ginger
- ¼ teaspoon ground allspice
- ¼ teaspoon ground nutmeg
- ½ teaspoon salt
- ½ cup (1 stick) room-temperature butter
- 1 cup packed dark brown sugar
- 1 large egg
- ½ cup pumpkin puree
- ¼ cup molasses
- 1 teaspoon vanilla extract

Preheat oven to 350°.

1. Line a baking sheet with parchment paper; set aside. Stir together the pumpkin pie spice and granulated sugar in a shallow bowl; set aside.

2. In a large bowl, whisk together flour, baking soda, baking powder, cinnamon, ginger, allspice, nutmeg, and salt. Set aside.

3. Using an electric stand mixer or hand-mixer on medium speed, beat together butter and brown sugar until light and fluffy, about 3 to 4 minutes. Add the egg. Beat until combined, about 30 seconds. Scrape down the sides of the bowl as needed.

4. With the mixer on low speed, add the dry ingredients and mix until just moistened, about 30 seconds. Refrigerate the dough for at least an hour.

5. Roll a heaping tablespoon of the dough into a 1½-inch ball (or use a 1½-inch cookie scoop). Roll the ball in the sugar mixture, and place it on the paper-lined sheet. Repeat with remaining dough, spacing balls about 2 inches apart. Gently flatten the balls using your fingers or a fork until they are about ¾ inches thick.

6. Chill the cookie sheets until it's time to bake each one. Bake one sheet at a time until the edges are set and cookies look cracked, about 10 to 12 minutes. Cool the cookies on the baking sheet for about 3 minutes, then transfer to the rack to cool completely.

REMAINS OF THE DAY

For those who think that Halloween is not for grownups, why not tap into your inner child—the part that remembers when holiday celebrations were more about fun than scratching off items on a to-do list? This year, cast off your inhibitions, don a costume, and head outdoors with a few "young-at-heart" friends for an afternoon of fun, food, and (yes!) fright. Dig up some bone-chilling décor, bring out a table and some seating, and allow our simple Halloween crafts, entertaining ideas, and easy-to-prepare snacks to prove that a kids-free party can be sweetly sinister.

*B*obbing for apples, pin the broom on the witch, and raucous games of hide and seek. Those are just a few of the squeal-inducing games that are played at children's Halloween parties everywhere. But what if you are past the age of treat bags and swinging a bat at a pumpkin piñata, yet still want to celebrate Halloween with a party? Invite some of your most spirited pals, assemble trays of sophisticated yet deceptively simple snacks and nibbles, and pull up a chair for an afternoon of light-hearted Halloween fun geared to your adult friends. Faux skull centerpieces, hanging skeletons that rattle in the autumn breeze, and bone-shaped bread set the stage for a round of macabre story-telling, blood-red wine sampling, and cackles of laughter as adults regale each other with tales of tricks played during Halloweens past. Make-ahead food and decorations contribute to the light-hearted, impromptu nature of the gathering, with recipes like Chocolate Graveyard Pie and Skull Candy Apples luring guests to the small, but tempting, buffet. A mix of sweet and savory hors d'oeuvres balances the rich flavors of the assembled red wine pairings: Bordeaux, Merlot, and Shiraz. As guests raise their glasses in tribute to your successful adults-only Halloween celebration, invite them to dust off their imaginations and share their talents for a round of spooky story-telling.

CREEPY CANDELABRUM
Scour antique shops and yard sales for ornate candle holders. Skeleton candles from the Halloween aisle of the crafts store will cast light on the gathering... unless bone-chilling winds pick up.

DOUBLE TAKE

A carved jack-o'-lantern is slit down the middle and fitted with a small, white, skull-faced pumpkin. Place a small battery-operated candle inside to back-light its impish grin.

OPPOSITE: Set the scene for a frighteningly good party with festive food and décor: **1.** A bowl of grapes and freshly-picked apples invite guests to nibble. **2.** A plastic skeleton hangs warily from a branch. **3.** A faux skull keeps watch over guests from its perch under a glass cloche. **4.** A deck of trivia cards, wrapped in skull-printed paper, is a fitting table favor.

PARTY FAVORS

Polished stones and small plastic skulls from the craft store nestle in a tiered stand filled with wrapped boxes of candies, playing cards, and trinkets.

CRANIAL CANDY

Fold scallop-edged craft paper over bags of licorice candy to serve as take-away gifts for the sweet-toothed adults in the crowd. We attached resin skull cameos—made using silicone molds from Etsy.com/Shop/Molds—to the paper tags using hot glue.

1

2

SPECIAL PRESENTATION

Spooky touches announce the theme: **1.** Find skull-themed invitations in the Halloween aisle of most craft stores. **2.** Guests will delight in baked brie topped with mincemeat. **3.** A pair of skeleton hands serves up store-bought cookies. **4.** Take-home favors in the shape of tiny wooden coffins from the craft store are painted black, filled with moss and bone candies, and topped with a cameo button.

3

4

INCREDIBLE EDIBLES

A selection of fine cheese and fruit fills a vintage pie plate. Guests will enjoy the savory sampler, which is complemented with a side of thin, crispy breadsticks and embellished with tiny plastic skulls.

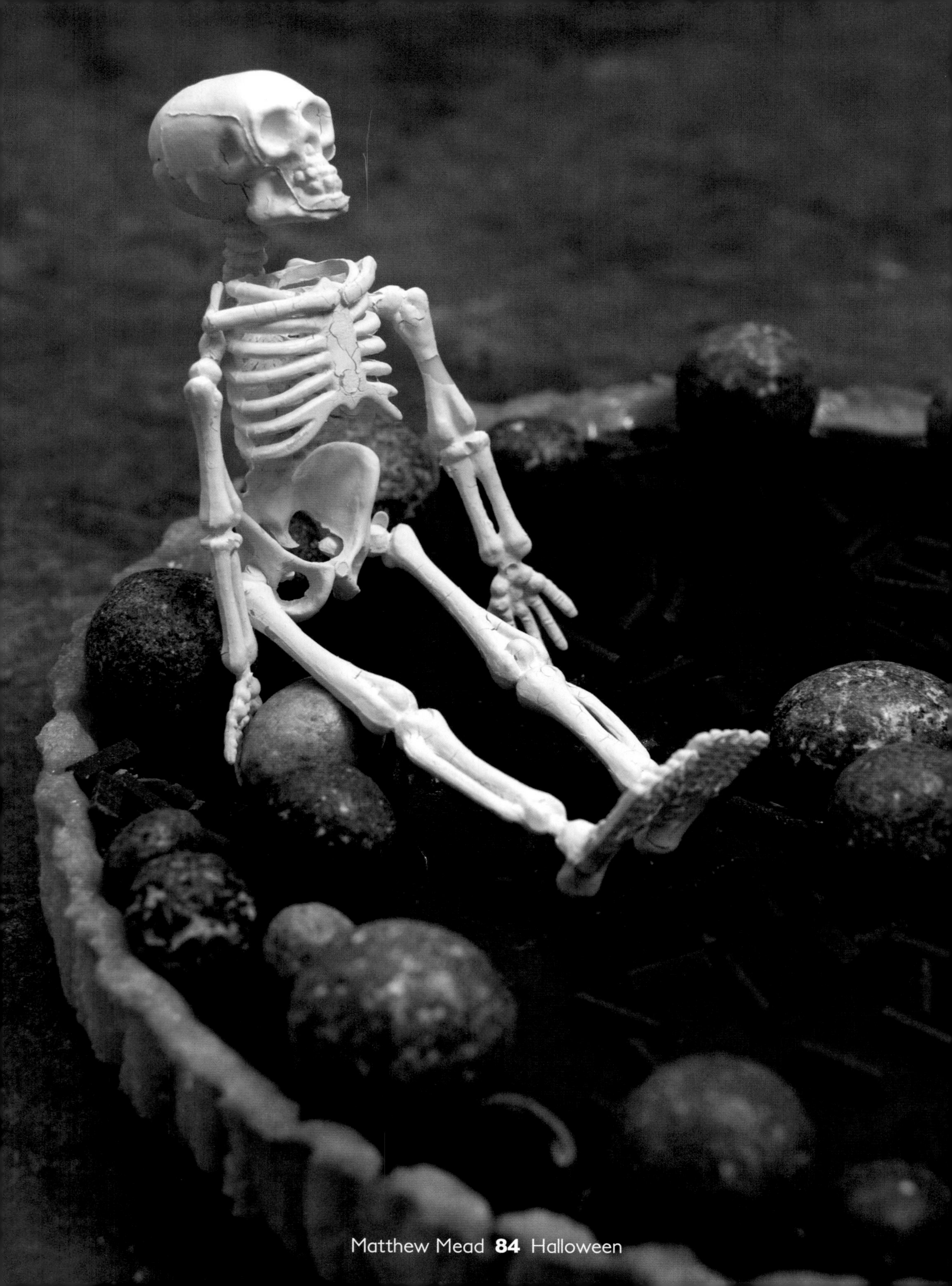

SO CEREBRAL

What could be more decadent or grown-up than wine and chocolate? A rich chocolate tart offers a smooth, chilled finish to an afternoon spent sipping wine and grape juice, nibbling on a variety of flavourful cheese, and sampling sweets like the Candied Apple Craniums (RIGHT). Guests will have no need to bone up on anatomy when spiny creatures like this Dollar Store skeleton takes center stage on top of the tart. Situated amongst chocolate rock candies (OPPOSITE), he looks as though he has just been unearthed from the chocolaty goodness. Float icy skulls in each juice glass (ABOVE) and watch as guests react to the unexpected grins as they take their first sip. Find all How-To directions beginning on page 88.

RUSTIC REFINEMENT

An outdoor Halloween celebration doesn't have to mean hay bales and scarecrows. Elevate the party atmosphere with tasteful décor and sophisticated styling: **1.** A cast iron pot from a local antiques store boasts intricate detailing and lends a sense of elegance to the rustic setting. **2.** A plush velvet runner—in a rich eggplant hue—strikes a regal note on the table, serving as a subtle reminder that this is an adult's party: no sticky fingers allowed! **3.** A small-scale bust is crowned in a sprig of Concord grapes.

HOW TO: GRAVEYARD PIE

WHAT YOU'LL NEED

- Store-bought chocolate tart
- Chocolate curls or jimmies
- Rock-shaped chocolate candy
- Two plastic skeletons
- Lollipop stick or skewer

1. Gather the tart-decorating supplies and embellish the top of the tart with chocolate curls or jimmies.

2. Arrange chocolate rock candies around the circumference of the pie. Fill in the center with several more candies, leaving room for the skeletons. Secure the lollipop stick through the back "bones" of one of the plastic skeletons. Insert the skeleton into the tart (OPPOSITE) until its feet lie flat atop the tart. Nestle the second skeleton in a seated position on top of the tart. Prop it up against larger pieces of the rock candy to ensure it won't topple over.

> "This Graveyard Pie gives a whole new meaning to the term 'death by chocolate.'"
> —Matthew

HOW TO: BONE BREAD

WHAT YOU'LL NEED

- Six rounds of Naan bread from the supermarket
- Olive oil
- Herbes de Provence
- Pastry brush
- Bone-shaped cookie cutter
- Black olives
- Dip

1. Use the bone-shaped cookie cutter to create the bread bones from the Naan bread. Arrange the bread bones on a tray and brush with olive oil; sprinkle with Herbes de Provence.

2. Place the bread bones onto a serving platter and serve with cream cheese and black olive dip (see recipe page 239). Use cut-up black olives to create a skull "face."

HOW TO: GOBLET GRAVE

WHAT YOU'LL NEED

- Greek yogurt
- Skull and cross bones ice cube tray
- Grape juice
- Goblet
- Spoon
- Spatula

1. Spoon the Greek yogurt into the ice cube tray. Use a spatula to smooth the top. Place in freezer overnight until firmly set.

2. Let the cubes soften in their tray for several minutes before removing. Place the cubes in a dish to serve (set the dish atop a decorative bowl filled with ice to keep cold). Add a skull and cross bones pair into the goblet of grape juice.

We used the Bone Chillers food-safe silicone ice tray from FredAndFriends.com to make these tasty cubes.

HOW TO: SKULL WATCHMAN

WHAT YOU'LL NEED

- ○ Old candlesticks or pieces of molding
- ○ Black craft paper
- ○ Plastic or papier-mâché skull from the crafts store
- ○ Small black hat
- ○ Hot glue gun and glue sticks
- ○ Scissors
- ○ Double-stick tape
- ○ Straight edge or bone folder

1. Use scissors to cut a sheet of construction or craft paper into three 2x3-inch pieces. Fold each piece of craft paper back and forth in a fanfold. To start the fanfold, fold one end over about ½ inch, using a bone fold as a guide. Turn the paper over and fold the end up; continue folding the paper in accordion-like pleats.

2. Use double-stick tape to adhere the edges of each of the three pleated fan sections together to form a circle.

1

2

3

3. Apply hot glue to the top of the candle stick and firmly press the fan down onto it until secure. Use more hot glue to secure the skull onto the fan and to attach the hat to the top of the skull (ABOVE). Make several skull watchmen and arrange them along the table as spooky sentries to guard over guests while they eat.

HOW TO:
CANDIED APPLE CRANIUMS

- ○ Six Red Delicious apples
- ○ Crab apple twigs
- ○ 12 ounces white chocolate wafers
- ○ Black fondant
- ○ Piping gel
- ○ New small paintbrush

1. Wash and dry the apples, and insert an apple twig firmly into the bottom of each one. Set aside.

2. Melt the white chocolate wafers in a medium-sized, heat-proof bowl over simmering water; stir occasionally.

3. Dip each apple in the melted chocolate and spoon the chocolate up onto the sides and top of the apple. Place each apple on a sheet of waxed paper until the chocolate is set.

4. Use a small knife or cookie cutter to create fondant eyes and a nose for each apple. With a small, new paint brush, apply piping gel to the back of each fondant feature and secure to the surface of the apple.

"Even 'big kids' become excited at the thought of biting into a candy apple, and white chocolate is always a hit."
—Matthew

SCAREDY CATS

Not only do they signal bad luck, black cats are sure signs there's something wicked in the air. Skip the witch and focus on her helpmate with this fun party that was inspired by vintage window decorations.

FELINE FLOUNCES

Stage a scene like no other this Halloween with black-cat-inspired decorations. Use their furry faces for tissue paper medallions, pumpkins, and cake toppers (THIS PAGE). The black and orange palette is easy to spin from table to wall—and even dangle from the ceiling (OPPOSITE).

PUPPET MASTERS

By painting stir-sticks black, you can turn the paper motifs—copied from vintage window decorations—into easy decorations and puppets. Give them as takeaway gifts when the party is over.

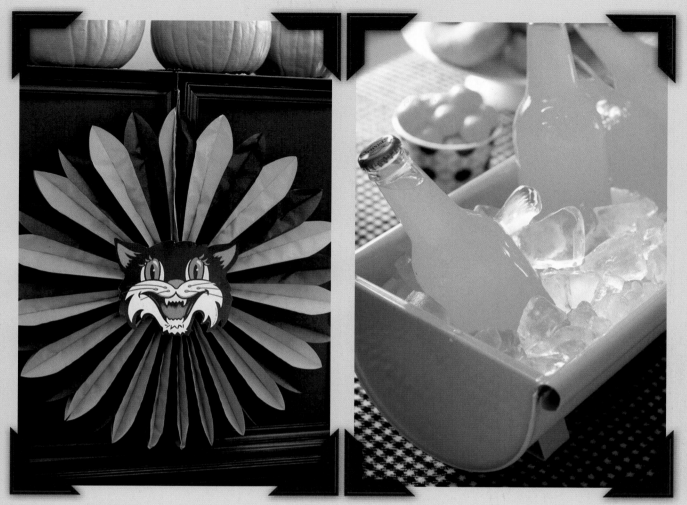

PARTY READY

Put your home in a spirited mood with tissue paper medallions purchased from a crafts store or party-supply store. To personalize them, attach a cat face to the center (ABOVE, LEFT) using glue dots. An orange-painted trough holds icy beverages that suit the color scheme (ABOVE, RIGHT).

You might not think to include a flea market in your list of stops when shopping for Halloween decorations. But Matthew does. Over the years, he has found some interesting and unusual things there. Some of the stuff he finds is instant material for a seasonal look, like masquerade masks and rustic lanterns, and some reveals its purpose over time. Old window decorations were like that. Used in the front windows and doors of homes from the 30s through the 70s, these paper motifs were slightly tattered and faded from use. Regardless, Matthew would snatch them up when he saw them, and eventually had a sizable collection. "We used to have them when I was a child, and I would beg to get them out shortly after school began in September," Matthew says. "I've always zeroed in on them at flea markets because of that feeling of excitement and anticipation." This year, he sifted out all the black cats and used their likenesses to stage a party for his co-workers and neighbors. "When you find them at thrift stores and secondhand shops, they're always inexpensive," Matthew says. "And they're usually somewhat damaged. I scan them into my computer and repair the images using a program like Photoshop®." You can download the cats used in this party from HolidayWithMatthewMead.com, and print them in a variety of sizes. Or, preserve the black ink in your printer and send them to a print/copy store to have them printed in color on heavy weight paper or card stock.

FAST AND FABULOUS

The amount of time it takes to set up for a party is always related to how much effort you're willing to go to. The ideas from Matthew's party are meant for picking and choosing. Do them all, or do just one. It's up to you! **1.** Hit the bulk candy aisle for anything edible that's the right hue. Pick one or two varieties, such as peanut-butter candies and gumballs, and offer loads of them by filling flowerpots and metal goody tins to the brim. **2.** Layer two tablecloths—black-and-white check over orange—for a festive look. Don't have tablecloths? Use yardage from the fabric store and don't worry about hemming. Or pick up a couple of plastic picnic cloths and trim a few inches off the bottom edge of the one you lay on top. **3.** You can turn a plain table or tablecloth into a themed one by adding circles cut from colorful papers. Trace around bowls or drinking glasses, or use a large scrapbooking punches to make multiple shapes. For the pennants, cut triangles from felt, which doesn't fray, and attach using glue dots. Small pinwheels are from the party supply store.

OPPOSITE: To set up a stunning buffet for the party, think high-to-low. Place the tallest decorations, such as pinwheels that hang from the ceiling or tiered dessert servers, at the back. Short items go in the front. At bottom level, tuck pumpkins or tissue paper poufs into the void where the tablecloth meets the floor.

Orange has been such a hot color of late, it's easy to find fabrics and accessories that fit a Halloween theme.

GOOD OMENS

Matthew's collection of vintage window cutouts (also called window die cuts) dates back to different eras. They are not particularly valuable, but the illustration styles are varied and interesting. Using the downloads on Matthew's web site, HolidayWithMatthewMead.com, you can print these same images, or you can look for your own window decorations at flea markets and online auction sites.

HOW TO: CUTOUT PUPPETS

- ○ Decorative cutouts or copies
- ○ Glue dots
- ○ Paint stirring sticks
- ○ Black acrylic paint
- ○ Paintbrush

1. Paint the stirring sticks black and let dry.

2. Attach two or three glue dots to one end of the stirring stick.

3. Attach the cutout to the stick using glue dots.

4. Display the figures in tarnished trophies (BELOW, LEFT), weather-beaten flowerpots, or any rustic old vessel. A little visible age on the container suits the vintage charm of the cutouts.

You can use these cutout puppets as outdoor decorations, too, by sticking them into pots of colorful mums.

HOW TO: KITTEN PUNCHBOWL

WHAT YOU'LL NEED

- Black paper
- White pencil
- Small scissors
- Clear double-sided tape
- Empty punch bowl or large fishbowl

1. Using the templates provided on page 253 or at HolidayWithMatthewMead.com, trace the features of a cat face onto black scrapbook or construction paper. You could also freehand draw the features.

2. Cut out the features and use double-sided tape to adhere them to the glass bowl. For best effect, let the ear tips extend above the rim of the bowl.

3. Fill the bowl with bright orange punch, juice, or Kool-Aid. Matthew likes the color—and taste!—of Tang.

HOW TO:
CUTOUT PUPPETS

WHAT YOU'LL NEED

- Decorative cutouts or copies
- Glue dots
- Tissue paper medallions like these from Bethany Lowe. Check Bethanylowe.com for a retailer near you.
- Colorful twine
- Art markers (optional)

1. Color-copy the decorative cutout and trim off any excess paper. Affix glue dots to the back of the cutout. Stick the cutout to the center of the medallion.

2. Use colorful string, twine, yarn, or ribbon to hang the medallion from the ceiling.

3. A less-expensive variation on this project is to copy the cutouts in black and white. Then add highlights and color in the features using art markers.

HOW TO:
EASY TOTE BAG

WHAT YOU'LL NEED

- 9x12-inch felt pieces (3 black, 1 yellow, 1 pink)
- Fabric scissors
- White fabric marker
- Fabric glue
- Embroidery floss
- Embroidery needle

1. Trace and cut a nose triangle from the pink felt. Trace and cut two eyes from the yellow felt. Trace and cut two black circles from one of the black felt pieces. From what remains of the black felt piece, cut two straps. Stack the whole black felt pieces and use fabric glue around three sides to seal them into a tote with an open top. Use more dots of the fabric glue to adhere the ends of the straps inside the upper edge of the tote. Let the glue dry.

2. Using more fabric glue, attach the felt face shapes the front of the tote bag.

3. Draw the cat mouth and whiskers using the white fabric marker.

4. If desired, add a border of blanket stitches to the top edge of the tote. Use white embroidery floss, or another color of your choosing, to add this embellishment. Not familiar with this beginner stitch? Visit HolidayWithMatthewMead.com for a link to a video that shows you how to sew a blanket stitch.

This project is easy enough for kids to enjoy. Older children can even add the decorative stitch detail.

NATURAL DISASTERS

Imagine the scene: You're walking in the darkening woods alone when you hear the snap of a branch and rustling leaves behind you. Your heart races and your knees grow weak just as your brain tells you to *run!* Mother Nature can be a scary chick. Gathering natural items from the woods is just the ticket for creating macabre Halloween scenes.

HUNT AND GATHER

To create an eye-catching vignette, gather stones, twigs, leaves, and moss during a nature walk. You can use them in a plethora of arrangement themes. Glass cases with birds and spider illustrations suggest a naturalist has collected fierce-looking items to study. Recreate a boggy scene with a toad casting garden ornament (OPPOSITE) and dried mushrooms as companions.

WATCHER IN THE WOODS

Every autumn, the natural world offers a bounty of supplies that are virtually free and accessible right outside your door. Branches, leaves, rocks, seedpods, and seashells can all be remained, as in this monster's laboratory scene (OPPOSITE). Hand-make a few creepy additions: The spider web, for example, is a template on page 245 and at HolidayWithMatthewMead.com. Other items, like this papier-mâché skull (ABOVE, LEFT), are easy to find in stores and online. At garden centers or on walks, look for rocks that have unusual textures and twigs that mimic other things; this twig looks like a grackle's talon (ABOVE, RIGHT).

W hat puts the creep in creepy? Your imagination. And if you turn to nature for your inspiration then you will never run out of great ideas. Begin by scoping out your backyard for fallen branches, leaves, pinecones, and seedpods. Next set up shop in a clean, dry place like a garage or basement to stage all your findings and begin the process of brainstorming what to create. Anything can be transformed— so take these cues to envision your natural supplies as other things, and you will unleash lots of possibilities. Use straightforward tools, such as paints, stamps, and glues to embellish and blend items with what you have on hand—computer-printed labels turn ordinary glass jars into spooky specimen cases, for example. Or use dried moss to stage a contoured sand dollar to look like a dehydrated brain. "I also like to paint rocks, twigs, and shells black to give them a dark look," Matthew says. "When something looks familiar but has a twist, it keeps guests wondering and curious, which is so much fun at Halloween."

CREEPY CRAFTS

Shadow boxes are fun ways to create tabletop focal points (OPPOSITE). Inside pre-made boxes from the crafts store, use a hot-glue gun to attach faux bugs. Line them up like a precious specimen display. For another box, press leaves flat inside the pages of a heavy book, then spray-paint them ghostly white. Draw on eyes on with black permanent pen. **1.** A super-simple idea is to rest gnarled twigs in the crack of a vintage nature book, opened to a vivid description. **2.** Create the look of taxidermy by placing fake blackbirds from the party supply or crafts store in a black case. Sprinkle on some birdseed for fun effect. **3.** Draw skulls and monster features on flat white stones using permanent marker. Glue magnets to the back so they can become kitchen decorations for a seasonal memo board.

PICKLED PUSSES
To make this showy display of preserved "friends," start by peeling the skin off firm, white-fruit apples, such as Granny Smiths. Then carve faces into the apple fruit using a paring knife. Highlight the features using black icing gel, then submerge them in vinegar in a jar.

CASE WORKER

For a vignette of sizeable proportion, stack glass displays, such as vintage library cases, old aquariums, or used science displays. Then stage multiple scenes using crafts-store birds, dried mushrooms from the grocery store, and painted eggs. Collect leaves from the backyard, press and dry them, then spray them white and add stamped designs in black ink.

PROVIDE A SPECIMEN

1. Spray a sand dollar black, and place it in a case with moss, which you can find in the floral aisle of crafts stores. **2.** Hand-paint or print a creepy spider image on sepia-color paper. (You'll find the template on page 245 and at HolidayWithMatthewMead.com.) **3.** Use a rubber stamp to put a skeleton's face on a flat stone from the crafts store or garden center. **4.** Hot-glue dried moss pieces to cover a blank foam head.

RING AROUND THE ROSEY

This decidedly ghoulish front-door wreath will spook friends and neighbors. Use hot-glue to attach seedpods, moss, twigs, and dried mushrooms to a sturdy wreath form, and then cover in cotton cobwebs.

Dragon
bone

DRIED ON THE SHORES
OF LAKE TRANSYLVANIA

DRAGONS OF A FEATHER

A nest of twigs and leaves and cotton cobwebs is the perfect roost for future fierce dragons. To make the eggs, use stone-texture spray paint to coat plastic or wooden eggs from the crafts store or dollar store. When dry, spray them green, and add daubs of brown paint with a brush. Cut paper wings from yellow paper, add details with colored pencil, and hot-glue them on. Look for the wings template on page 244 and at HolidayWithMatthewMead.com.

HOW TO: GHOSTLY LEAVES

WHAT YOU'LL NEED

- ⭕ Tree leaves
- ⭕ Heavy books
- ⭕ Paper towels
- ⭕ White spray paint
- ⭕ Seasonal rubber stamps
- ⭕ Black stamp ink

1. Sandwich collected leaves between paper towels, and place under a stack of heavy books. Let the leaves dry and flatten for at least two days and no more than a week. Lay them on newspaper, then spray-paint them white. Let dry and spray the other side.

2. Press seasonal stamps into black ink and use them to decorate the white leaves.

Maple leaves allow the most space for stamped motifs, but you can use any shape or variety that you find appealing.

MARVELOUS MANTELS

Dressing your mantle for Halloween doesn't have to mean filling your cart at the seasonal pop-up store. Gather recycled items from around the house and create a most stylish focal point that will charm your friends with its industrious nature. Here, items from your home are arranged in bold color palettes for three distinct Halloween looks.

RECYCLED STYLE

Newspaper, aluminum foil, glass vessels, and a black handled shopping bag all unite to create fun and spooky settings for your holiday mantel. Glass bottles and jars filled with colored water (OPPOSITE) line the ledge, and their fun faces (made of black paper) boast cheeky grins.

Spray planters and vases with your favorite paint shade and tuck in some lollipops for an unexpected display.

3

JAR FACE

Just about anyone can rustle up some empty jars, loose candy, and water to create a whimsical mantel display: **1.** Black paper can be cut into triangles and other shapes to create jack-o'-lantern faces. Use double-stick tape to adhere them to the glass or pottery. **2.** Fill a vase with Sahara® floral foam; insert lollipops into the foam and top with mixed candy. **3.** Amass a collection of jars and fill them with water that has been mixed with orange food coloring to create colorful backdrops for the funny faces. Fill a pitcher with water and add drops of coloring to achieve the desired hue. Stir to blend until you are happy with the shade.

BLACK WATCH

Elegant silver pieces mix with stark black silhouettes to create a sophisticated mantel display. Black and white always makes a dramatic statement and this mantel embraces theatrics to achieve its look. Black paper, recycled from a handled gift bag, is cut into shapely silhouettes—while newspaper is folded into a graphic medallion. Find the silhouette templates on page 247.

SHARP CONTRAST

A black and white palette naturally comes to mind when selecting a Halloween color scheme. Its striking contrast plays on the relationship between good and evil—like friendly ghosts and haunting vampires. **1.** Black and white striped muffin cups cradle mini white faux gourds for a dressed up look. **2.** Newspaper is folded into several fans, attached together to form a circle, and then embellished with a black paper party plate and a vintage black and white photo. **3.** A spooky Dracula silhouette appears to hover hauntingly above the scene, striking a foreboding presence. Use Zots® to attach him to a mercury glass candlestick. Find the template on page 248.

Ghosts and bats are created from brochure printer paper, aluminum foil, twine, and beads. We used a mix of old clear and yellow glasses to perch paper bats and curvy ghosts on simple skewers. Bowls and glassware filled with colorful candies or topped with miniature pumpkins further enhance the sense of fun the arrangement evokes.

TWO BY TWO

1. Foil bats are cut from paper that has been fused to aluminum foil. We used Zots® to attach them to foil-wrapped skewers—creating the illusion that they are flying above the scene. **2.** Ghosts can be cut from the templates found on page 247. Reproduce the curvy shapes using the template and sturdy printer paper, which will enable the paper ghosts to stand tall in the colorful glasses. **3.** Elevate real or faux pumpkins atop miniature cordial or shot glasses to create varying heights and interest. **4.** Use a length of black twine to create a garland filled with foil bats that have simply been taped on. A single foil-wrapped bead on each ends finishes off the garland.

HOW TO:
MANTEL SILHOUETTES

WHAT YOU'LL NEED

- Vases, bottles, and/or jars
- Silhouette templates (find on page 247)
- Black craft paper and black paper bag
- Scissors
- Double-stick tape and Zots®
- Tinfoil

- Brochure paper
- Spray adhesive
- White gel pen
- Small wooden beads and black string
- Skewers

1. Print off the pumpkin features templates from page 247 and cut out using small, sharp scissors. Use double-stick tape to adhere them to the bottles, jars, and vases.

2. Print and cut out the silhouette templates. Place them atop the black gift bag and trace around the shapes with a white gel pen. Use scissors to cut out the shapes and use Zots® to apply them to a mirror on your mantel—or use double-stick tape to secure them to sturdy brochure paper for a stand-up effect.

3. Print the ghost template onto matte-finish brochure paper; cut out. Slip the ghosts inside glasses and line them up along the mantel.

4. Print the bat template and cut out. Adhere aluminum foil to brochure paper with spray adhesive. Trace the bat template onto the foil and cut out. Use a Zot® to adhere to a foil-wrapped skewer or stick several along a black cord using double stick tape to make a garland. String foil-wrapped wooden beads in between each bat, and at the end of the cord to finish.

PUTTIN' ON THE DOG

In some homes, when parents talk about dressing up their kids for Halloween they are talking about their four-legged children. With a bit of fabric and supplies like an old bed sheet and simple craft tools, you can whip up some surprisingly easy costumes to bring Halloween panache to your pooch.

W hether trick-or-treating with your kids, greeting visiting ghosts and goblins at your door, or customizing an invitation for an upcoming Halloween gathering, outfitting Fido in a costume and showing him off will make him the leader of the pack. While stores have entire aisles devoted to such wardrobes, making a dog costume is more economical and (scouts honor!) easy to do. A hard and fast rule? Consider comfort: Choose the costume (and its construction) based on your dog's collar. If she is used to wearing one, then any friction or pulling in this area won't be as distracting—increasing the likelihood that the pup will keep the costume on. If your dog wears sweaters and jackets, then a cape will be a good choice. Ideally, make the costume ahead of time and try it on your dog a few minutes each day so that he's used to it by the time Halloween rolls around. And while he or she prances around looking adorable, have your camera at the ready to capture some images for a treasured greeting card or invitation.

KENNEL CLUB

Elsie, a Shar Pei (OPPOSITE), is transformed into a winged bat with the help of wire and craft foam. Oscar, my Yorkshire Terrier (ABOVE), sports a simple cape and a doll-sized witch's hat.

WHAT BIG EYES YOU HAVE

Juniper, a Basenji mix, is used to wearing sweaters, so casting her in the role of Little Red Riding Hood was genius. A soft ribbon gathers a red velvet fabric remnant from the fabric store. We used the finished edge of the fabric to create the head and tail of the costume, and used iron-on fusing to finish the sides. This no-sew costume just needs to be tied to the collar to stay in place. Leave the cape about two inches short of the tail.

DOG-EARED

Colby, a Yellow Lab puppy, donned an old sheet for an instant quick change from pup to ghost. Measure your dog while he stands and cut the fabric, tapered from front to back, so that the costume isn't dragging on the ground.

AYE, AYE MATEY

Sometimes a hat will do the trick. Cooper the King Charles Cavalier looks commanding as a pirate of the sea. His long locks are reminiscent of rebel sailors of the briny deep.

DOG TREATS

Dressing up your dog is 90-percent illusion. Pick just the right items and the effect is seamless. Lila, an Italian Greyhound, is a slight and elegant figure who looks very fitting in feathers. Craft a boa from the crafts store into angel wings with some light-weight wire. Attach wings to a dog harness at the back of the dog's neck and from the mid-section strap using cotton ribbon.

HOW TO: PUPPY WITCH

WHAT YOU'LL NEED

- ½-yard black mircrofiber fabric
- Doll-size witch hat
- Scissors
- Awl
- ½-yard black ribbon or black tinsel garland

1. This classic costume is easy to make with microfiber fabric, which does not fray. For a dog the size of Oscar, Matthew's Yorkshire terrier, you'll need to cut a rectangle of fabric that is about 11x14 inches. Size the rectangle roughly to the size of dog you have, then trim later.

2. Two inches from the top of the fabric, cut eight holes spaced about a ¼ inch apart. Thread ribbon through holes and gather. Tie cape onto the dog's collar. Trim fabric to suit the size of the dog, with the end of the cape falling 2 inches above the tail and the sides short enough not to drag on the ground. Using the awl, punch a hole in each side of the hat. Thread with remaining ribbon and tie under the chin of the dog. Or, tie the hat to the collar of the cape so it rests on the dog's back.

Depending on the fabric color and hat style, you can use this technique to dress a witch, vampire, or devil.

HOW TO: PIRATE HAT

WHAT YOU'LL NEED

- ○ 8½x11-inch piece of brown felt
- ○ Glue gun
- ○ Buttons

1. This no-sew hat is reminiscent of a child's newspaper hat. Fold felt in half lengthwise. From the fold, fold each corner into the middle to form a triangle. Hot-glue under the corners to secure. Fold the bottom flap up on each side and glue the undersides to secure. Glue buttons to the center of the hat as an emblem.

2. Soft felt is pet-friendly and easy to work with. If you wish, you can make up several caps for different personalities: In white, the cap looks like a nurse's topper; or, add a feather to a green hat to become Robin Hood.

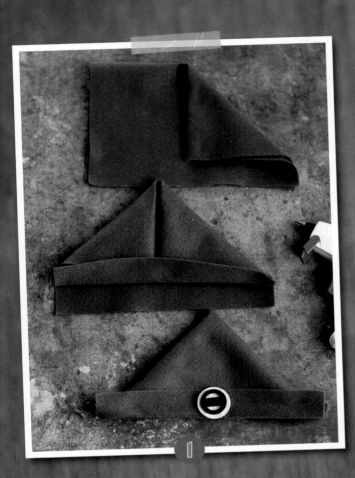

Try out these costumes a few days or weeks before the holiday to get your pet accustomed to wearing them.

HOW TO: ANGEL WINGS

WHAT YOU'LL NEED

- 50-inch piece of 18-gauge wire (used for jewelry-making)
- 1 white feather boa
- Wire cutters
- Cotton ribbon
- Silver floral wire

1. Bend the wire in the middle, and then from the middle bend two matching arches like the shape of a Valentine's heart. Bend the end of the wires back to the inner point of the heart and twist ends together; this creates the form for the wings. Wrap the wire form with the feather boa until covered. Attach ribbon to the center of the two wings and tie it to the dog's harness.

2. White feathers are a natural fit with the fur of this Italian greyhound, but you can fashion feathers from any color boa you wish.

HOW TO: WINGED BEAST

WHAT YOU'LL NEED

- 2 11x17-inch sheets of black fun foam
- 30-inch piece of 18-gauge wire (used for jewelry-making)
- Glue gun
- Scissors

1. Cut each piece of fun foam in half lengthwise. Cut the pieces in the shape of bat wings, to make four wings, or two pairs of identical wings. Pair two of the matching wings, and sandwich one end of the wire between them. Glue the sandwich together. Glue the other pair of wings to the other end of the wire in the same manner.

2. When the glue is dry, bend the exposed wire in the middle over your dog's back and secure it to a harness if necessary.

To turn this hat into a gargoyle headdress, form horns out of paper clay and meld them to a pet-size headband.

HOW TO: LITTLE RED RIDING HOOD

WHAT YOU'LL NEED

- ¾-yard red velvet fabric
- 1-yard coordinating ribbon
- Scissors

1. Starting at two corners on one side of the fabric, use scissors to cut slits at regular intervals in an arcing line from one corner to the other, with the mid point reaching about 8 inches from the edge of the fabric. Thread ribbon through the slits; this will form the hood.

2. Tie the ribbon loosely around your dog's neck, and trim off any extra ribbon. Check the cloak's overall length and cut off excess fabric so your pooch doesn't get tripped up.

Cutting a generous hood helps it stay on—even over tall, alert ears.

HOW TO: SPECTRAL POOCH

- Fabric tape measure
- 1 white cotton sheet
- 1 piece black construction paper
- Black marker
- Scissors

1. Using the fabric tape measure, circle your dog's head at the widest part of his or her jaw. Take note of the measurement, and use it as the perimeter measurement to cut out a template from black construction paper. Elongate the oval as necessary to fit your dog's head shape. Trace around the template onto the sheet, using the black marker. Cut out the shape.

2. Slip the sheet over your dog. Trim off excess fabric at the point where it brushes the ground.

DEVILISH DONUTS

Looking for a delicious treat to serve to your favorite ghosts and goblins? Try these quick and easy ideas for embellishing store-bought donuts. You can offer them up at a party, or just dish up a frighteningly good after-school snack.

SCARE TACTICS

Appeal to your naughty side with this chocolate cake donut (OPPOSITE). Fill the center with cherry pie filling, add a devils-food frosting tail (piped from a plastic baggie with the corner snipped off) and serve it with a "pitchfork." For this Bavarian cream skele-treat (THIS PAGE), poke eye holes in a marshmallow and cut a slit for the mouth. Press in candy-coated pumpkin seeds for teeth and black dragées for the eyes and nose.

MUNCHKIN OWL
Almost too clever to eat, this donut-hole owl can feed
a crowd of hungry trick-or-treaters. See step-by-step
assembly instructions on page 153.

THE EYES HAVE IT

Another fast way to plate a bunch of scary snacks is to buy a dozen chocolate cake donuts. Mix up a quick icing using bright green candy coating, melted and drizzled over the donuts. Add candy eyes, which you can find online and in the cake-decorating aisle of the crafts store.

SPICE POPS
Turn donut holes into caramel apples by inserting cinnamon sticks. For extra deliciousness, dip them in melted butterscotch chips and add a swirl of melted white chocolate.

treats

GHOUL ENOUGH TO EAT

1. Tie up a bundle of crullers using kitchen twine, and add a fiery center with tinted frosting. To get the flame striations, squirt streams of orange and yellow gel food coloring to line the pastry bag, then fill it with white frosting. **2.** Place a royal icing ghost on a donut glazed with a cloudy mist of white icing. Look for similar decorations in stores that sell cake-decorating supplies. **3.** Slice a chocolate donut in half, then pipe in white boiled icing. Add a dusting of crumbs from crushed chocolate sandwich cookies. **4.** Walk the plank into the briny deep with caramel donuts dusted with fleur de sel.

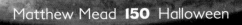

BEWARE OF VAMPIRES

Take a stack of donuts from bland to mind-blowing (OPPOSITE) when you leave hints of a vampire's visit. Poke two fang holes in the tops of honey-glazed donuts, then dribble some red gel food coloring out of the holes and down the sides of the donut.

CREEPY CRAWLIES

More cute than chilling, this spider is a cinch to put together. For the body, use a chocolate frosted Bavarian crème donut, with a cake donut head. Donut holes form the legs and eyes. Use large chocolate chips, anchored in dots of yellow-tinted frosting, to make the eyes pop. If needed, you can use more of the frosting like glue to keep the donut holes from rolling away.

FINGER-LICKING TRICKS

If you can squish a marshmallow and melt some chocolate, then you can transform a simple donut into a wildly fun treat. The techniques are simple enough to have little helpers give you a hand.

HOW TO MUNCHKIN OWL

WHAT YOU'LL NEED

- 15 plain donut holes
- 10 powdered sugar donut holes
- 14 chocolate-glazed donut holes
- 2 Filled donuts and 2 plain cake donuts
- White frosting in a plastic zip-close bag
- Brown construction paper
- 2 dark chocolate melting wafers

1. Follow this pattern to form the body of the owl out of plain donut holes.

2. In the same manner, fill in the legs and wings using chocolate and powdered sugar donut holes.

3. Stack the cake donuts on the filled donuts to create the eyes, and then fill in the centers with white frosting piped from a plastic bag with the corner snipped off.

4. Complete the look by cutting feathers from brown construction paper and placing chocolate melting wafers on the eyes.

DRESS-UP AND DESSERTS

Nothing beats the mystery and drama of a masquerade party. Here's an idea for a stress-free get-together that has all the fun of a fancy affair but requires minimal work for the host. Set out moody decorations, focus on just sweet treats—your choice whether they are freshly baked or store-bought—and invite your guests to parade the night away.

ON THE DARK SIDE

Stage shadowy scenes around the house using dark backdrops—black or midnight blue fabric yardage draped over tables, shrouding windows, or simply tacked to the wall behind an array of black objéts (OPPOSITE). A bust wearing a mask, which is simply a satin ribbon with slits cut for eyeholes, melds with flameless candles, a fake crow, and vintage broaches for sparkle. Fold a paper cone and fill it with chocolates for guests to take home (ABOVE, LEFT). Nestle flameless candles in cocktail glasses or candleholders and pour in black icing sugar to dampen their glow.

*H*alloween dress-up fun doesn't have to be reserved just for children. But rather than ask friends and neighbors to show up in elaborate getups (that Big Bird costume gets so hot!) invite them to simply don masks, which you can provide in a basket by the front door. Set the party hours for late in the evening, after the trick-or-treat madness has subsided and people feel more relaxed—or better yet, hold it apart from Halloween Eve, such as the weekend before. Array a variety of desserts for everyone to sample and enjoy, and offer coffee, tea, cider, or something stronger. By keeping the mood casual, you will feel less harried, and guests will appreciate your gentle hospitality.

PARTY PROWESS

Here are some tips for party-hosting success: For a narrowly defined party, such as desserts only, you'll want to provide a variety of treats that appeal to every taste. This spice cake, for example, is for guests who don't care for chocolate. For decorations at a gathering where guests are likely to mingle and move about, place smaller touches in every room. Push a table against a wall to keep it out of the flow of traffic (OPPOSITE), and arrange rustic garden urns and candles with a few spooky elements, such as fake spiders. Prop up a flea-market portrait and attach a ribbon mask with double-sided tape.

CLEVER & TASTY IDEAS

Some people like to bake; others prefer to create the decorations. Pick your favorite party-hosting chore, and buy the rest at the store. The same goes for effort: These suggestions make for a cohesive and fun masquerade party. You can do them all or just choose to do your favorites. All the recipes are available on page 238, and on HolidayWithMatthewMead.com. **1.** Ice cream floats bring out the kid in us all. Tuck in stirrers that are topped with bats cut from black scrapbook paper. **2.** This after-dinner take on a cheese ball uses peanut butter and it's rolled in chocolate and peanut butter baking chips. Serve it with crackers and thin cookies. **3.** A cheesecake is always a decadent treat. Add a spider web using chocolate frosting.

OPPOSITE: Create an eerie scene by covering up the numerals in a wall clock (as if time has been erased) with your menu and tucking in a flameless candle.

Colonial Spice Cake
Creamy Coffee Float
White Chocolate Cheesecake
Peanut Butter Bliss
Gingerbread Cupcakes
Pretty Puffs
Floating Ghost Cookies

CAKE WALK

For the chocolate lovers at the party, set a cake frosted with white icing on a cake stand. It can be store-bought or homemade as you wish. Surround it with chocolate crumbles (which you make by freezing a candy bar, then hammering it with a rolling pin or the edge of a saucepan), and top it with a mask.

HOME PLATES

For this themed place setting, put a clear salad plate on top of a dinner plate with a decorative black pattern around the edge. In between the two, sandwich a circle of black paper decorated with a spider web drawn using a white fine-line marker. Make silverware service a cinch by binding together a full set in a black napkin, wrapped in ribbon and accented with bare twigs.

WEE TREATS

A festive party offering, cupcakes reinforce your theme and are easy-to-grasp servings. Make them yourself using the gingerbread cupcake recipe on page 238 and at HolidayWithMatthewMead.com. Or visit a gourmet cupcake bakery in your area to pick a tasty seasonal flavor. Tuck in plastic bat decorations to customize the look to suit your party.

MORE MAGICAL TOUCHES

These embellishments make a party special: **1.** Fill a cake stand with flameless candles and arrange strands of cotton cobwebs or quilt batting to look like smoke. **2.** Print out customizable place cards at HolidayWithMatthewMead.com, then anchor them in vintage broaches. **3.** Set fake crows to guard a bowl filled with cream puffs from the bakery. **4.** To make these ghosts, cover Stella D'Oro® breakfast treats with white frosting and add eyes using a black gel frosting.

HOW TO: FLOATING GHOST COOKIES

WHAT YOU'LL NEED

- ○ 1 9-ounce package Stella D'Oro® Breakfast Treats Original Cookies
- ○ 1 16-ounce canister vanilla frosting
- ○ 1 .75-ounce tube black gel frosting

1. Place the breakfast treats on a wire rack, and place the wire rack on a piece of parchment or wax paper to catch drips. Take off the lid and put the frosting canister in the microwave. Microwave on 50-percent power for 1 minute, then stir and microwave another 30 seconds, or until it is soft and pours easily. Use a spoon to drizzle the frosting over the breakfast treats. Let dry.

2. Using black gel frosting, place small dots on one end of each breakfast treat to create eyes.

You'll find gel frosting anywhere you buy cake-decorating supplies. The tube's fine tip makes detail work easy.

HOW TO: WEB FROSTING

WHAT YOU'LL NEED

- 32 ounces milk chocolate chips
- Medium glass mixing bowl
- Plastic squeeze bottle, clean and empty
- Funnel

1. Remove the cheesecake from the pan. Place chocolate chips in the bowl in the microwave, and heat at 50-percent power for 1 minute. Stir the chips, and then heat for 30 seconds more. Stir and repeat at 30-second intervals until most of the chips are melted. The remaining chips will continue to melt after you remove the bowl from the microwave. Pour the chocolate into the plastic squeeze bottle, using the funnel if necessary.

2. To create the web pattern, squirt four lines across the cake, intersecting in the middle. Then draw shorter lines connecting each long line, starting in the middle and working out.

The melted chocolate web hardens as it dries, giving the creamy cheesecake a crunchy topping.

MAGIC SHOW

Gather a crowd of thrill seekers for an afternoon of magic tricks, fortune telling, and board games. A sunny autumn day and an outdoor setting keeps the mood light and allows ample space for younger guests to burn off some of the excitement in the days leading up to Halloween.

CAUTIOUS APPROACH

Guests can pull up a chair and seek their fortune at this light-hearted party that appeals to those who seek out the "trick" in trick-or-treating. Stacks of pumpkins offer unspoken warnings to fortune seekers.

run!

hid.

Curious things is what Magic brings.

scary

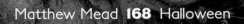

WARNING SIGNS

Large orange pumpkins, sporting stick-on words of caution, line the stone steps in the garden (ABOVE, RIGHT). Vintage party props—like these old playing cards and spectacles (ABOVE, LEFT)—rest atop a chalkboard-painted table.

*H*alloween is a much anticipated time of year and the build-up can be painstaking for little ones. Why not stretch out the celebration by hosting an outdoor party that allows friends to gather, kids to run around, and offers a fun day filled with snacking, playing games, and admiring everyone's pumpkin carving skills? A large backyard, field, or park can serve as the perfect place to party on a sunny weekend afternoon before the big day. Invite guests to bring along a carved pumpkin and hold an informal pumpkin judging event. Encourage aspiring magicians to try out their best trick, and enjoy being outside in the autumn sun—admiring the leaves, playing games of tag, and returning to the party tables for simple snacks, spirited board games, and some amateur fortune telling. Easy-to-make decorations, like the clock face garland (OPPOSITE), can be created during an afternoon craft session and add to the fun of organizing the event. Find the template to make your own clock garland at HolidayWithMatthewMead.com.

BITS AND BITES

Stock up on simple treats: **1.** A wire-mesh star holds a chocolate pumpkin and sugary gumballs—to be doled out as guests leave. **2.** Stretch a fabric butterfly mask over a glass vase filled with M&M'S®. **3.** Toss pistachios with three drops of orange food coloring for a colorful alternative to candy. **4.** Tiny Halloween boxes are filled with temporary tattoos.

MAGIC TRICKS

Set a spooky scene with these easy tricks of the trade: **1.** Wooden Halloween ornaments, found at a craft store, hang from a bewitching little tree fashioned from a Manzanita branch. Painted black and inserted into the top of a small pumpkin, the crooked, spiky branches can be found in the dried flower section of many craft stores. **2.** For a simple but striking pumpkin centerpiece, hollow out a pumpkin and cut an opening in its front. Rest a spooky ornament—like this bronze owl statue found at a flea market—on the edge of its opening and light it up with a battery-operated candle. **3.** Ornate images from an old book or encyclopedia can be scanned into your computer and printed onto a sheet of vellum. Secured over the carved opening of the pumpkin using tacks, it is a sophisticated alternative to the traditional jack-o'-lantern.

OPPOSITE: A seasonal vignette is created using a vintage cat-shaped planter, lamp base, and miniature cauldron filled with sprigs of bittersweet.

Curious things is what *Magic* brings.

CURIOSITIES
A coat of chalkboard paint gives an old drop-leaf table new life as a spot to play board games, hear one's fortune, or "sit for a spell." Write a message on its front to inspire guests to get into the spirit of the party.

CARD TRICKS

A deck of black and white playing cards fills a vintage loving cup. Traditionally given out as a trophy to an event winner, this two-handled cup doubles as the perfect centerpiece for a games table.

TRICKED OUT

Have fun with party props: **1.** A well-traveled suitcase, covered in wizard-themed travel stamps with a decidedly Harry Potter vibe, holds prizes for game winners. Find the wizardly stamp templates on page 240. **2.** Scan an old photo and print it onto vellum for a spooky pumpkin face. **3.** A ceramic tree trunk mug holds soda pop. **4.** Time games with an hourglass.

CHECKMATE
An old chess board was hauled out of storage and put into play for the party. A scattering of M&M'S® provides sugary sustenance for players pondering their next move.

BLACK CAT
A black cat arching its back is carved into the front of a pumpkin to brighten up a stone wall. A coat of black paint makes the silhouette pop against the yellow background. Find the directions on page 180.

WISE OLD OWL
Keep an eye out for owl-themed décor and ornaments, like this ceramic statue found at a thrift shop and given the symbolic task of watching over the party.

HOW TO:
PAINTED PUMPKIN

WHAT YOU'LL NEED

- ○ Pumpkin
- ○ Pumpkin carving kit
- ○ Cat template (template at HolidayWithMatthewMead.com)
- ○ Black and yellow acrylic paints
- ○ Two small paint brushes
- ○ Wood carving tools
- ○ Sharpie® or permanent marker
- ○ Thumb tacks

1. Cut around the top of the pumpkin and scoop out the contents of the pumpkin until scraped clean. Cut out the cat template and secure it to the front of the pumpkin using thumb tacks. Trace around the template using a Sharpie® or permanent marker.

2. Remove the template and carve around the shape of the cat using the wood carving tool, cutting into the pumpkin about ¼-inch, and etching away the flesh until the surface is smooth (eyeball the circular "frame" around the cat).

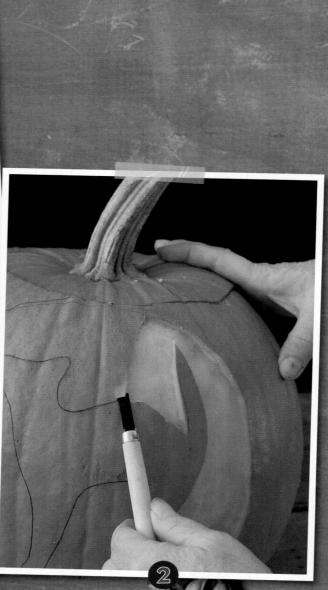

3. Use a small paint brush to paint the circle surrounding the cat a bright yellow. Let dry.

4. Paint the cat shape black using a fresh paint brush. Once dry, lift off the top of the pumpkin and insert a battery-operated candle into the pumpkin to illuminate the cat silhouette.

"Pumpkin carving brings out my competitive side: I challenge myself every year."
—Matthew

HOW TO:
PUMPKIN GALLERY

WHAT YOU'LL NEED

- ○ Pumpkin
- ○ Pumpkin carving tools
- ○ Scissors
- ○ Face template (see page 249)
- ○ 8½ x 11-inch sheet of vellum (find in the scrapbooking or art paper aisle of the craft store)
- ○ Black thumb tacks or push pins
- ○ Black Sharpie® or permanent marker
- ○ Battery-operated candle

1. Cut a circular opening in the top of the pumpkin, set the lid aside, and scoop out the contents of the pumpkin until clean. Cut out a rectangular-shaped window in the face of the pumpkin and scrape any pulp strings away.

2. Print out a Halloween image (using our template on page 249) onto vellum paper. Cut out the vellum image to fit the rectangle opening. Pin it in place using thumb tacks or pins. Use a permanent marker to draw a free-form frame around the image. Place a battery-operated candle inside the pumpkin to light up the vellum photo.

SWEET ART

Like the rainbow of paints a fine artist uses, edible pigments, powders, and metallic dusts bring delicious masterpieces to life. Ply them on plain candies and lollipops to create one-of-a-kind Halloween treats.

To find the colorful materials used to transform these plain candies, stroll the cake-decorating aisle of the crafts store, visit a bakery supply store, or shop online. The investment is tempered because the pigments, powders, and glitters last several seasons and can be used to decorate anything edible, from cookies to cupcakes to pies.

WHAT YOU'LL NEED

- Edible color dust in green, orange, yellow, purple, black, and brown edible glitter
- Edible gum paste
- Plain white chocolate lollipops and figures
- Empty wide-mouth glass jars
- Clear cellophane bags
- New, clean paintbrushes, make-up applicators, and cotton swabs

Depending on where you shop, you'll find these bright food embellishers called color dusts, color powders, icing powders, or edible pigments.

①

②

③

④

⑤

1. You can make your own candy pops using molds and white-chocolate candy melts from the crafts store, or buy them already formed.

2. To color this jack-o'-lantern, use angled brushes—one for each color—to poke the edible color dust into small holes and crevices.

3. Take the lid off a wide-mouth jar, and stick a ball of edible gum paste to the center of it.

4. Prepare the gum paste to hold the lollipop stick by poking a hole with a bamboo skewer.

⑥ **⑦**

⑧

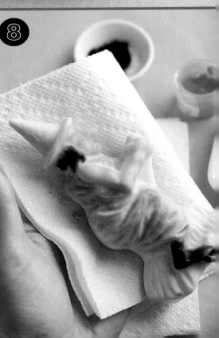

5. Fill the lid with seasonal candies, such as candy corn.

6. Screw the jar onto the lid to create a dome, and add a fake plastic or candy spider for creepy effect.

7. A hollow chocolate witch stands up on her own, but you can add a bit of gum paste to the bottom if needed to hold her to the jar lid.

8. There are two techniques to add the color dusts to plain candies: apply them dry with a cotton swab or make-up applicator, or mix them into a small amount of almond or lemon extract and paint them on with a paintbrush.

PRESERVATION SKILLS

Decorated candies in glass jar scenes like these are excellent take-away gifts at parties. Or enlist help from young artists to decorate the candies, then present them to grandparents or a favorite teacher. Individually wrapped frog pops (OPPOSITE) are perfect for trick-or-treaters who come to the door, and they make good classroom treats, too.

Paint frog candies with green and yellow paints, then sprinkle on edible glitter while paint is still tacky. When dry, slip them into cellophane bags.

CREEPY CURB APPEAL

Be the best house on the block with simple but showy Halloween decorations that are sure to attract a crowd of trick-or-treaters to your door.

PUMPKIN PARADE

A vintage metal owl (OPPOSITE) can be outfitted with a candle to glow at twilight. Perch him by the door to greet guests. With just a bit of thought, and a sturdy step-ladder, you can add Halloween panache to your porch entryway (BELOW).

PUMPKIN PORTRAIT

A wooden frame is painted black and glued to the front of a pumpkin. Add a twig from outside and a cut-out black silhouette, and you have an instant design that involved no carving or removal of pumpkin "guts."

FESTIVE TRIMS

Black poster paper, punctuated with cut-out paper stars (we traced around cookie cutters to make them), becomes a spooky faux stained-glass window treatment (ABOVE, LEFT). Oversized round paper medallions (ABOVE, RIGHT) are hung like bunting from the porch roof. Secure them to the porch molding using easy to remove three-dimensional glue dots.

Decorating your home for Halloween is a bit like baiting a mouse trap with cheese: To be the most talked about house on the street you have to use colorful and engaging decorations that catch the eyes of passersby and draw in trick-or-treaters. We turned to simple paper party decorations from Bethany Lowe designs (visit BethanyLowe.com for a retailer near you) and recycled some garden planters and ornamentation into striking décor pieces for the porch. "Use what you have on hand" is a mantra often chanted by Matthew, and this porch design is no exception. "Eye-catching décor doesn't have to be complicated to achieve an effect that is truly magical," he says. "If you can't pull it together in just about an hour's time then you might be working a bit too hard." To deck out the porch's entry (see page 191), an oversized garden urn became the perfect place to stash a mix of treats for neighborhood children, and unique pumpkin personalities can be created with a little paint and supplies from the craft store. "I like simple," says Matthew. "You can decorate a pumpkin in many ways without sharpening up the kitchen knives." Indeed, a collection of crafts, garden implements, and natural supplies will allow you to create a Halloween theme that showcases your home—and announces to the neighbors that "fun lives here."

HELP YOURSELF

A round piece of glass is set atop a large planter or garden urn to make an instant table. An owl planter-turned-treat dispenser holds court alongside colorful napkins and a festive Halloween cake that is sure to satisfy the sweet tooth of rowdy trick-or-treaters.

Have your family help decorate and line the
porch with their personalized jack-o'-lanterns.
Transform a pumpkin (BELOW) with an easy
henna-inspired design. Create your own pattern
and fill in the design using black puffy paint.

ITSY BITSY SPIDERS

An orange clay pot, cleaned out of its faded fall blooms, is filled with black river stones and topped with black spiders painted white. Fill several to line the walkway leading up to the porch. When dusk arrives, the addition of battery-operated candle votives will help light the way.

STEP RIGHT UP

Details matter with just about every decorating project, and decking out your front porch is no exception: **1.** A white Jack-Be-Little pumpkin, with the addition of a pair of watchful eyes (see how-to directions on page 59), weighs down napkins that might get caught in a howling wind. **2.** An owl planter sets the scene: Place a plastic liner inside each plant holder and fill with foil-covered and cellophane-wrapped candies and chocolates. **3.** Painted, decorated pumpkins are perched atop black stations made using turned curtain rods found at a home center. Mount the rods on a tiered platform and top with a pumpkin.

OPTICAL ILLUSION

Look to nature when decorating pumpkins. **1.** A small urn sports an owl made using dried flowers, seeds and a paper beak. **2.** A chalkboard-painted watering can speaks of a "watery grave." **3.** Fill an orange pot with foam, Spanish moss, and faux succulents painted black for a scary botanical statement. **4.** Bring a tipsy pumpkin to life with some feathers, feet, and eyes.

CHALKBOARD CHARM

Anything round can become a jack-o'-lantern. Use chalkboard paint to transform an old globe, and draw on your favorite chalk face. Add a jaunty flourish with a vintage top hat, secured in place using Zots®.

HOW TO: HENNA PUMPKIN

WHAT YOU'LL NEED

- ❍ Three-dimensional black puffy paint
- ❍ Faux pumpkin
- ❍ Pencil or pen
- ❍ Images of henna designs or your favorite fabric pattern

1. Print off henna designs from the internet, or follow the design of your favorite fabric (our pattern was inspired by fabric made in India). Use a pencil or pen to mark out the pattern onto the surface of the pumpkin.

2. Working from the top of the pumpkin down, use three-dimensional puffy paint to fill in the design. Let dry overnight.

If you're willing to try a freehand approach, your design is limited only by your imagination.

HOW TO: BIRD SILHOUETTE PUMPKIN

WHAT YOU'LL NEED

- Pumpkin (real or faux)
- Thin, wooden scrolled frame (find in the wood-working aisle of a crafts store)
- Black acrylic paint
- Small paintbrush
- Small twig
- Black craft paper
- Scissors
- Hot glue gun and glue

1. Paint the wooden frame and twig black; let dry. Using black craft paper and the bird template on page 249, cut out the shape and use hot glue to secure it to the center of the pumpkin.

2. Hot glue the wooden frame onto the pumpkin, ensuring the bird is centered within the frame. Use more hot glue to adhere the twig to the base of the bird silhouette.

HOW TO:
PUMPKINS TAKE FLIGHT

WHAT YOU'LL NEED

- High quality artificial flowers from the craft store
- Fresh chrysanthemum blooms
- Pumpkins (real or faux)
- Package of black craft feathers
- White pumpkin seeds
- Black acrylic paint and paint brush

- Wired plastic bird feet (removed from a Dollar Store bird or crow)
- Chestnuts and pinecones (two of each)
- Craft paper and scissors
- Florist's wire
- Hot glue gun and glue

1. Turn the pumpkin on its side so that its stem becomes its nose. Use hot glue to apply chrysanthemum blooms for eyes. Poke a black feather into each side of the pumpkin to give it "wings." Use push pins or hot glue to secure the top hat to the pumpkin. Place the pumpkin bird atop a mini gourd, block of wood, or a book and inset the bird's feet into the bottom front of the pumpkin for legs.

2. Paint clean, dry pumpkin seeds and pinecones black. Once dry, use hot glue to adhere the black pumpkin seeds onto an 8-inch length of florist's wire that has been bent into a curved V-shape. Cut out a diamond shape from craft paper and paint black pupils onto the center of two chestnuts; set aside. Cut most of the stems off of two faux blooms and insert the remaining stems into the pumpkin where each eye should go. Use hot glue to attach the eyes, paper beak, pumpkin seed eyebrows, and the pinecone ears.

"Decorate using items that you already have, nature's offerings, or easy-to-find supplies at the crafts store."
—Matthew

②

POLTERGEIST PARTY

Set a twilight meet-up with friends at a local graveyard for an unforgettable Halloween activity. Tell real or make-believe ghost stories, and then go on a hunt for apparitions. Afterward, convene to share your findings and enjoy some ghoulish treats.

IN THE MOOD

Mark the start of the scavenger hunt with a reference to a local or imagined figure. A black cape and top hat (OPPOSITE) suggest the ghost of Ichabod Crane is nearby. As the evening grows dark, offer lanterns to scavengers. Color copies of grim-looking portraits inserted in the side panels of lanterns offer spooky illumination.

If allowed, scatter décor around the cemetery (on benches or public tables— never grave markers) to highlight spots on the tour or scavenger hunt. This grouping combines a head from a resin garden statue with a wood architectural medallion, gourds, moss, and cabbages. Blackberries are set out to attract crows.

STRAIGHT FACES

At flea markets, it's common to find old photo albums and framed portraits. Make copies of somber faces (or download these from HolidayWithMatthewMead.com) and use them for table decorations or take-away gifts. Scan and reduce the size so the faces fit in a crafts-store bracelet (ABOVE, LEFT) or in a napkin ring (ABOVE, RIGHT). Use découpage medium to seal the papers to the metal.

There's nothing quite like a scavenger hunt to fuel fun competition. As fans of the numerous ghost-hunting shows on reality TV know, when you add the challenge of finding a few spirits of the departed, you have a spine-chilling way to enjoy a fall evening with game friends. Before he set up this activity, Matthew contacted the trustees of his local cemetery and asked permission to gather there. It's always important to make contact with the governing board, church administration, parks department, or cemetery caretakers to get permission for your activity and learn the hours the cemetery is open to visitors. "Some cemeteries provide maps of notable graves, or of local historical figures, facts, and dates," Matthew says. "These can be incorporated into your scavenger hunt or used for a tour."

Cemetery etiquette dictates that you do not touch grave markers, stay on walkways and paths, clean up after yourselves, be considerate of other visitors, and take care to preserve plantings and memorials. Pictures are usually allowed, but ask permission first.

"If your local cemetery is off-limits to visitors, ask the local historical society or library for ghost stories that are set in your town," Matthew says. "You could take a tour of haunted houses instead."

SCENE SETTERS

Set up decorations at the cemetery, or at a park nearby. **1.** A pile of white pumpkins, gourds, and cabbages suit the low-key color palette. **2.** A glass orb rests on an alabaster candlestick. **3.** Crafts-store moss wreaths encircle the broken head of a garden statue. **4.** An old lock and key set suits the theme of the get-together.

GATHER AND HUNT

Washing a plain table in thinned gray paint mimics the color of the aged stone tombstones. Fill it with goodies, snacks, or takeaway gifts, or simply arrange fall decorations that create the right mood.

SPIRIT-DETECTING KIT

When the hair stands up on the back of your neck or you pass through a spot of cool air, pull out one of these ghost-hunting "instruments": vintage magnifying glasses an old barometer, or anything that looks like a scientific tool.

GHOST HUNTING KIT

OUTDOOR DÉCOR

Use these décor ideas for a party, or just stage them around your home and yard for rich, autumnal flavor. **1.** Cobbling together found bits and pieces, Matthew put a rusty iron candelabra on top of a metal urn, then placed mini white pumpkins where the candles should go. A stack of tarnished trays shows off musky mushrooms and gourds. **2.** This fetching scene is a spooky cemetery set out in miniature. Place candlesticks, urns, small statues, and trophy bases on a footed metal tray, then fill in with dried branches, berries, moss, and nuts. **3.** A humorous touch, this metal bust figurine—probably a finial from an old gatepost—wears a bulging headpiece.

CAKE TOPPER

Perhaps one of the most unusual cake decorations you'll ever pull together, this yummy chocolate cake from a local bakery wears ghostly green frosting. Tucked into the top are old photos on bamboo skewers and cleaned cremini mushrooms from the grocery store. Place it all on a stack of metal trays to give it elevated prominence.

COFFEE SERVICE

Celebrate a successful hunt and discuss poltergeist sighting with coffee and cake. Make your own seasonal treat, or purchase a pumpkin cake roll from the bakery.

RECORD KEEPERS

Personalize plain black journals with spooky highlights of the graveyard tour. With permission, take photographs of monuments and markers and then print and tape them to the front of the journals. You can also download these photos at HolidayWithMatthewMead.com.

GHOST JOURNAL

HOW TO:
GHOULISH JOURNAL

- Plain journal
- Tombstone photograph from Holidaywithmatthewmead.com
- Printer paper
- Scissors
- Double-sided tape
- Letter decals

1. Make a copy or print out the image of the tombstone. You can print it in color or black and white, as desired.

2. Cut out around the tombstone.

3. Place pieces of double-sided tape to the back of the image and adhere it to the cover of the journal.

4. Add letter decals to inscribe a message or personalize the journal.

Older tombstones wearing age or a coating of moss make the most interesting photographs.

HOW TO: GHOSTLY LANTERN

WHAT YOU'LL NEED

- ○ Lantern with removable glass panes
- ○ Copies Of old portraits, downloaded from Holidaywithmatthewmead.com and enlarged to fit
- ○ Vellum sheets
- ○ Scissors
- ○ Black spray paint
- ○ 3-inch pillar candle or battery-operated wickless candle

1. Gather your materials before you start. If the lantern is not black, remove the glass panes and spray it with black paint in a well-ventilated area. Let dry.

2. Using one of the glass panes as your guide, cut a portrait as well as a piece of vellum to size. Repeat for the remaining sides of the lantern.

3. Place the portrait on the outside of the glass pane, facing out, and then place the vellum over the portrait. Insert a glass pane-portrait-vellum sandwich in each side of the lantern.

1

2

3

4. Insert the candle, and light it if necessary. If you plan to walk with the lantern swinging in your hand, place some glue dots under the candle to keep it from sliding.

DUST TO DUST

Remember when you used to skip recess to draw on the classroom chalkboard and clap the erasers? Well, chalk art is here to stay—and you don't have to seek permission to unleash your inner Halloween artist.

*S*ince the invention of chalkboard paint, there has been nary an item or object that can't be recast as an art surface. And what better excuse than the celebration of Halloween to swath a slew of items in chalkboard paint and release your inner Van Gogh? Chalk art is fun, not permanent, and even the youngest members of the family can try their hand at it. A light-hearted holiday like Halloween offers up plenty of inspiration to try out a familiar art form—one that allows you to jump in feet first with only a piece of chalk and a paper towel to wipe away mistakes. Chalk art gives you the licence to create something new—everyday if you want to. To begin, purchase a can of black chalkboard paint in a quart or spray can. Gather objects or surfaces that you wish to use as decoration and then cover them in several coats of the paint. Once dry, you are free to illustrate the canvas in whichever design you desire. Your projects can be as wild and varied as you like: If you make a mistake, a quick swipe of an eraser allows you to begin the process anew—allowing for a virtually endless parade of one-of-a-kind art.

CHALK MARKS

A decorative, everlasting cement pumpkin (ABOVE) received a coat of chalkboard paint and some stylized designs, inspired by a wizard's cape. An antique cannon ball (BELOW) is enlivened with a visage of the moon.

KINGDOM COME

Any frame can become a chalkboard with a ¼-inch plywood insert painted with chalkboard paint. Illustrate in a fun theme like "keys to the kingdom"—which might include a dungeon key, a key to Pandora's box, or even a spare key. We Googled keys and found numerous illustrations to inspire our ornate tools of entry.

HOOT HOOT

Revive a dated and overly cutesy porcelain figurine from the 70s with a new "cool" vibe by painting it black and highlighting just some of the details with chalk. You can find many similar figurines at yard sales, flea markets, and thrift shops for as little as a quarter.

DRAWN AND TIERED

A cupcake stand receives scrolling embellishments and is topped with a chalkboard-painted mannequin. Highlight the face with chalk and cap with a witch's hat; dress the top tier with giant white gumballs to mimic a strand of pearls. Lower tiers hold cupcakes topped with wooden plant stakes that have been painted and illustrated with spooky eyes.

VARIATIONS ON A THEME

It's all in the details: **1.** A vintage pith helmet boasts an ever-changing imprint of graphic style. **2.** The eyes have it as these plant stakes peer out from atop a cupcake. Use black icing gel to paint the end that is inserted into the cake. **3.** A "chalkboard cookie" bears a spider that appears ready to crawl up the stand. **4.** Paint recycled bottles white and outfit them with a chalkboard label and doll-sized witch hats.

ALL THROUGH THE HOUSE

Virtually any surface can be an informal canvas: **1.** Chalk cloth moves chalk art to softer surfaces (see directions on page 228). **2.** Add whimsy to an old bureau's drawers with wizard-inspired words. **3.** Fear your reflection in this vintage mirror, edged and punctuated with a warning. **4.** An old birdcage in the shape of a dollhouse becomes a haunted Victorian with Halloween-inspired gingerbread details.

PAN MEETS KETTLE

Old iron kitchen staples, like frying pans and tea kettles, need no painting; their rough porous surfaces readily welcome chalk designs. Just wipe with a damp cloth when Halloween is over.

Flee

or

FRY

HOW TO: OWL PILLOW

WHAT YOU'LL NEED

- Chalk cloth
- Owl template
- Scissors
- Binder clips
- Poly-filling
- Chalk
- Sewing machine
- Heavy-duty thread

1. Print the owl template (find it at HolidayWithMatthewMead.com) and place it atop the chalk cloth. Trace around the pattern using chalk; cut out the shape and set aside. Cut two rectangular-shaped pieces of cloth and join them together (allowing a 1-inch overlap) using binder clips to secure the overlapped edges.

2. Set the cut-out cloth owl atop the rectangular pieces (wrong sides together) and use chalk to outline the shape of the owl along the inner edge.

3. Use a sewing machine to sew the two sides of the pillow together. Use scissors to trim the excess cloth from the pillow shape.

4. Stuff the pillow with poly-filling until you achieve the desired fullness. Tip: a flatter pillow will make for an easier surface upon which to draw the design.

5. Use the owl image on page 250 as a guide to draw on your chalk design.

HOW TO: SPOOKY SUGAR COOKIES

WHAT YOU'LL NEED

- Round and square sugar cookies (sized to fit each design)
- Royal icing
- Icing spatula
- Kitchen scissors
- Edible Halloween wafer papers

1. Order Matthew Mead's exclusive Halloween cookie wafer papers from FancyFlours.com. Assemble your supplies.

2. Cut out the wafer papers and set aside on a flat, dry surface. To achieve the scalloped edges, purchase wafer cookie cutters at FancyFlours.com. Prepare your favorite royal icing recipe and spread a thin layer of the icing onto the cookies; carefully place the Halloween wafer papers on top. Let set until the icing is firm.

Each edible wafer paper from Fancy Flours® is printed with USDA-approved food coloring on paper made from potato starch.

GET FANCY
Edible wafer papers transform everyday, ordinary cookies into miniature works of art. Sally Robinson and her team at Fancy Flours® create a variety of seasonal vintage images, botanical prints, toile patterns, and antique postcard reproductions—perfect for just about any kind of celebration you can imagine.

SOW A TASTY
PUMPKIN PATCH

Sure, ghosts and ghouls are fun to feature in Halloween decorations and festivities. But some of us prefer the lighter side of the holiday and don't have the stomach for scare tactics. As a centerpiece of your celebration, try this friendly cake, which showcases autumn's bountiful harvest in an appealing way. It's so simple to make and embellish, young children can help with planting—and eating!—the crop.

WHAT YOU'LL NEED

For the cake:
- ○ Chocolate cake mix, plus called-for ingredients
- ○ 9x12-inch baking pan
- ○ Cooling rack

For the topping:
- ○ Medium-size glass bowl
- ○ Small saucepan
- ○ Wooden spoon
- ○ 10 ounces bittersweet chocolate, finely chopped
- ○ 12 ounces heavy cream
- ○ 1 tablespoon butter
- ○ Chocolate wafer cookies, finely crumbled

For the pumpkins:
- ○ Clementines or small tangerines
- ○ Wooden skewer
- ○ Fresh cilantro or parsley leaves

Starting with your favorite chocolate cake mix makes this an easy-to-prepare holiday treat.

①

②

③

④

1. Start with a bag of tangerines or Cuties® clementines, and choose 10 to 11 fruits.

2. Pick some fresh cilantro leaves. If you don't like the heavy fragrance of cilantro, you can substitute milder Italian flat-leaf parsley instead.

3. To make the oranges look like vine-ripened pumpkins, remove what's left of the fruit's stem, and poke a hole using a bamboo skewer. Select a stem or two of the herb, and insert it into the hole.

⑤

⑥

⑦

⑧

4. Bake your favorite chocolate cake mix in a 9x12-inch baking pan, according to package directions. Matthew prefers Pillsbury Moist Supreme® devil's food cake mix. While the cake is cooling to room temperature, crush chocolate wafer cookies, such as Nabisco® Famous Chocolate Wafers, until you get about a cup of fine crumbs. You can put the cookies in a plastic zip-close bag and mash them with a rolling pin, or you can break them down in a food processor.

5. A shiny layer of chocolate ganache coats the top of the cake and looks like moist soil. To make it, place chopped bittersweet chocolate in medium bowl. Heat the heavy cream over medium heat until just boiling, and immediately pour it over the chocolate. Let the cream and chocolate sit for a minute, then stir the mixture with a wooden spoon until it's well combined. Add the butter and stir again until the ganache becomes creamy and fully mixed. Let it sit for 10 to 15 minutes until thickened.

6. Spread the ganache over the cooled cake in an even and smooth layer.

7. Using a large spoon or your fingers, sprinkle the cookie crumbs all over the cake.

8. To make this recipe for a crowd, bake up individual cupcakes, which are easier to serve. Top each one with ganache, cookie crumbs, and its own "pumpkin."

9. A paper scarecrow cutout is the perfect final touch. Create your own, or follow the template on page 249, and at HolidayWithMatthewMead.com. Tape the scarecrow to a black plastic drink stirrer or a bamboo skewer.

Make up a quick fizzy punch by stirring a cup of fresh-squeezed orange juice into a liter of orange-flavored seltzer water.

GINGERBREAD CUPCAKES

For the cupcakes:
- ○ 1½ cups all-purpose flour
- ○ 2 tablespoons ground ginger
- ○ 2 teaspoons ground cinnamon
- ○ ¼ teaspoon ground cloves
- ○ ¼ teaspoon ground nutmeg
- ○ 1½ cups unsalted butter (3 sticks), room temperature
- ○ 1½ cups granulated sugar
- ○ 3 tablespoons unsulphered molasses
- ○ 4 large eggs, room temperature
- ○ 1 teaspoon vanilla extract
- ○ 22 3-inch gingerbread men

For the frosting:
- ○ 1 8-ounce package cream cheese, softened
- ○ 3 cups confectioner's sugar
- ○ 2 teaspoons vanilla extract
- ○ 2 teaspoons cinnamon

Adjust oven rack to lower-middle position and preheat to 350° F.

1. Line a muffin pan with baking cup liners and set aside.
2. In a large bowl, sift together flour, ginger, cinnamon, cloves, and nutmeg; set aside.
3. In the bowl of an electric stand mixer fitted with the paddle attachment, beat the butter and granulated sugar until light and creamy, about 3 minutes. Beat in the molasses until incorporated. Beat in the eggs, one at a time. Beat in vanilla. Switch the mixer to low speed and gradually add the flour mixture. Mix until just combined.
4. Fill the baking cup liners three-quarters full, making sure that the batter is divided evenly. Bake cupcakes for about 30 minutes, or until a toothpick inserted in the center of them comes out clean. Let cupcakes cool in the pan for 10 minutes, then transfer cupcakes to a wire rack to cool completely.
5. To make the frosting, beat the cream cheese and confectioner's sugar until smooth. Add cinnamon and vanilla extract and beat until combined.
6. Place frosting into a large piping bag fitted with a 1M decorating tip. Pipe a spiral of icing, beginning at the outer edge of each cupcake and working inward. Dust with black icing sugar if desired.

COLONIAL SPICE CAKE WITH MAPLE CREAM CHEESE FROSTING

For the cake:
- ○ 3 cups all-purpose flour
- ○ 3½ teaspoons baking powder
- ○ 2 teaspoons pumpkin pie spice
- ○ 1 teaspoon baking soda
- ○ ½ teaspoon salt
- ○ 1½ cups granulated sugar
- ○ ¾ cup (1½ sticks) butter, softened
- ○ 3 large eggs
- ○ 1½ cup canned pumpkin purée
- ○ ½ cup evaporated milk
- ○ ¼ cup water
- ○ 1½ teaspoons vanilla extract

For the frosting:
- ○ 11 ounces cream cheese, softened
- ○ ⅓ cup butter, softened
- ○ 3½ cups confectioner's sugar
- ○ 2 to 3 teaspoons maple extract
- ○ Squeeze of lemon juice

Preheat oven to 325° F.

1. Grease two 9-inch round cake pans and set aside.
2. Combine flour, baking powder, spice, baking soda, and salt in a small bowl.
3. In an electric stand mixer fitted with a paddle attachment, beat sugar and butter until creamy. Add eggs, one at a time; beat for 2 minutes. Beat in pumpkin, evaporated milk, water, and vanilla extract. Switch the mixer to low speed and gradually add the flour mixture. Spread evenly into prepared cake pans.
4. Bake for 30 to 45 minutes, or until a toothpick inserted comes out clean. Cool in the pans on wire racks for 15 minutes; remove cakes from pans to cool completely.
5. To make the frosting, beat together cream cheese and butter until smooth. Gradually add in the confectioner's sugar and beat until fluffy. Add in the maple extract and lemon juice. Mix well. Refrigerate until needed.
6. To assemble the cake, cut each cake layer in half horizontally with a long, serrated knife. Spread frosting between each layer and on top of the cake and the sides.

WHITE CHOCOLATE CHEESECAKE

WHAT YOU'LL NEED

For the crust:
- 1 9-ounce package chocolate wafer cookies
- 6 tablespoons butter, melted and cooled

For the filling:
- 3 8-ounce packages cream cheese, softened
- 3¾ cups cold milk, divided
- 3 3-ounce packages white-chocolate flavor instant pudding mix
- 3 cups whipped topping, thawed

1. To prepare the crust, place a few cookies at a time in a food processor and process until they are fine crumbs. Pour crumbs into a medium bowl and add melted butter; stir with a fork until well combined. Press the mixture into the bottom and up the sides of an 8-inch spring form pan
2. Place the crust in the refrigerator to harden for about and hour.
3. In a large mixing bowl, beat cream cheese and ¼ cup milk with a whisk until well blended. Add remaining milk and dry pudding mix; beat with a whisk for 2 minutes. Using a wooden spoon, stir in whipped topping until well blended.
4. Remove the crust from refrigerator and fill with cheesecake mixture. Refrigerate for 4 hours until firm. Remove from refrigerator and remove cake from spring form pan.

ROYAL ICING

WHAT YOU'LL NEED

- 1 pound powdered sugar, sifted (4½ cups)
- 3 tablespoons meringue powder
- ½ teaspoon cream of tartar
- ½ cup warm water
- 1 teaspoon vanilla extract

1. In a medium mixing bowl, whisk together the powdered sugar, meringue powder, and cream of tartar. Add the water and vanilla extract; beat with an electric mixer on low speed until combined. Beat on high speed for 7 to 10 minutes, or until the mixture is very stiff. Refrigerate in an airtight container for 2 to 3 days.

PEANUT BUTTER BLISS

WHAT YOU'LL NEED

- 1 8-ounce package cream cheese, at room temperature
- 1 cup confectioner's sugar
- ¾ cup creamy peanut butter
- 3 tablespoons packed brown sugar
- ¾ cup milk chocolate chips
- ¾ cup peanut butter chips

1. In a large mixing bowl, beat cream cheese, confectioner's sugar, peanut butter, and brown sugar using an electric mixer until blended.
2. Spoon the mixture onto a large piece of plastic wrap; bring up all four corners and twist tightly, forming into a ball shape.
3. Place mixture in the freezer for about 1 hour and 30 minutes, or until it's firm.
4. Place peanut butter and chocolate chips in a flat dish. Remove plastic wrap from ball, and roll ball into morsels to completely cover, pressing morsels into the ball if necessary.
5. Place ball on serving dish; cover and freeze for 2 hours or until almost firm. Note: This recipe can be made ahead. Thaw at room temperature for 20 to 30 minutes before serving.

CREAM CHEESE-AND-BLACK OLIVE DIP

WHAT YOU'LL NEED

- 1 8-ounce package cream cheese, softened
- ½ cup reduced-fat sour cream
- 1 4-ounce can chopped black olives
- ¼ cup finely chopped onion
- ¼ teaspoon garlic powder
- ¼ teaspoon cayenne pepper, to taste

1. Mix everything together until thoroughly blended.
2. Serve or chill until ready to serve.

CREAMY COFFEE FLOAT

WHAT YOU'LL NEED

- 1 cup milk
- ½ cup ice cubes
- 2 teaspoons granulated sugar
- 1 teaspoon instant coffee granules
- 3 scoops vanilla ice cream
- ½ teaspoon of cocoa powder

1. In a blender combine milk, ice, sugar, and coffee, and blend until frothy and well combined. Pour the mixture in a tall glass and add ice cream. Top it with sprinkles of cocoa powder.

Trade Secrets templates p. 8

HALLOWEEN KIT

MAGIC POTIONS
(handle with care)

Pest Control
template p. 14

Magic Show templates p. 166

School of Wizardry

Bug juice

Squashed from bugs
that live on a
S P R U C E...
filtered and sieved
to make a
JUICE.

C A U T I O N

MAGIC SPELLS

Creatures from the Deep template p. 38

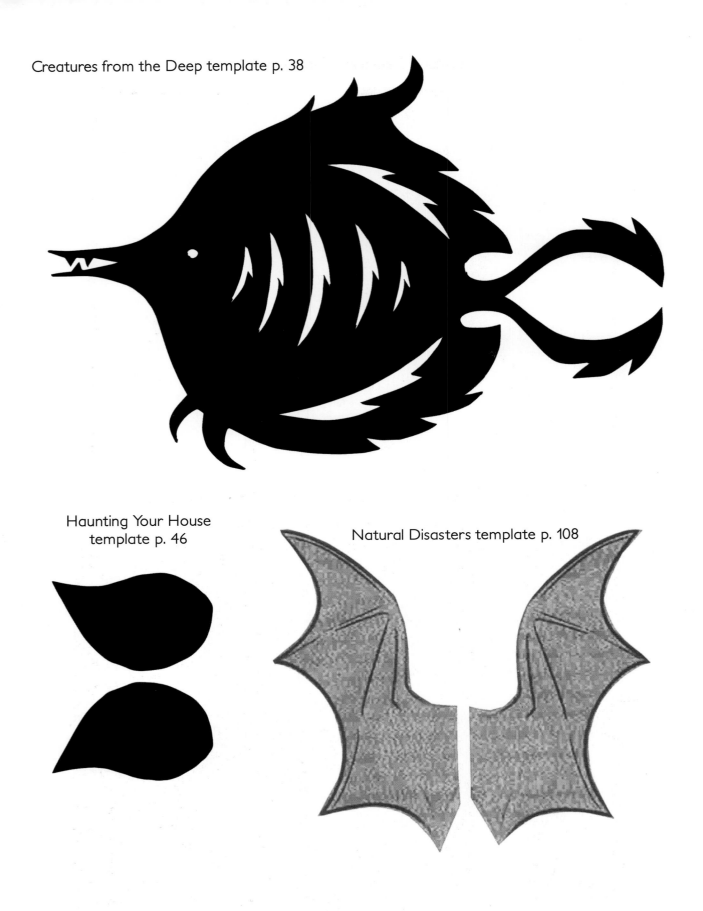

Haunting Your House
template p. 46

Natural Disasters template p. 108

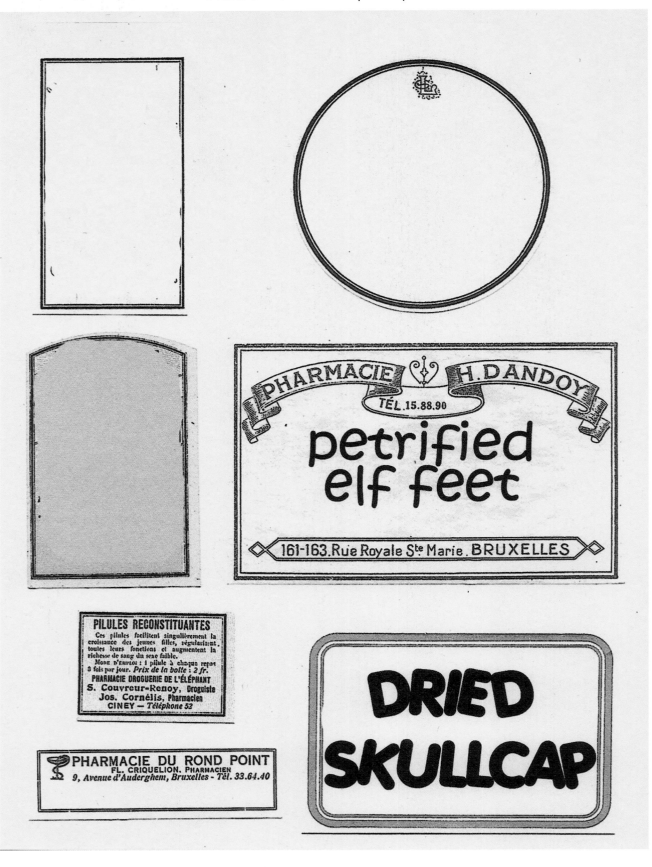

Marvelous Mantels template p. 122

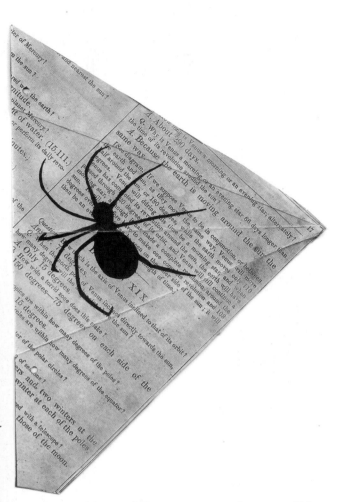

Dress Up and Desserts templates p. 154

Magic Show template p. 166

Creepy Curb Appeal template p. 190

Sow a Tasty Pumpkin Patch template p. 232

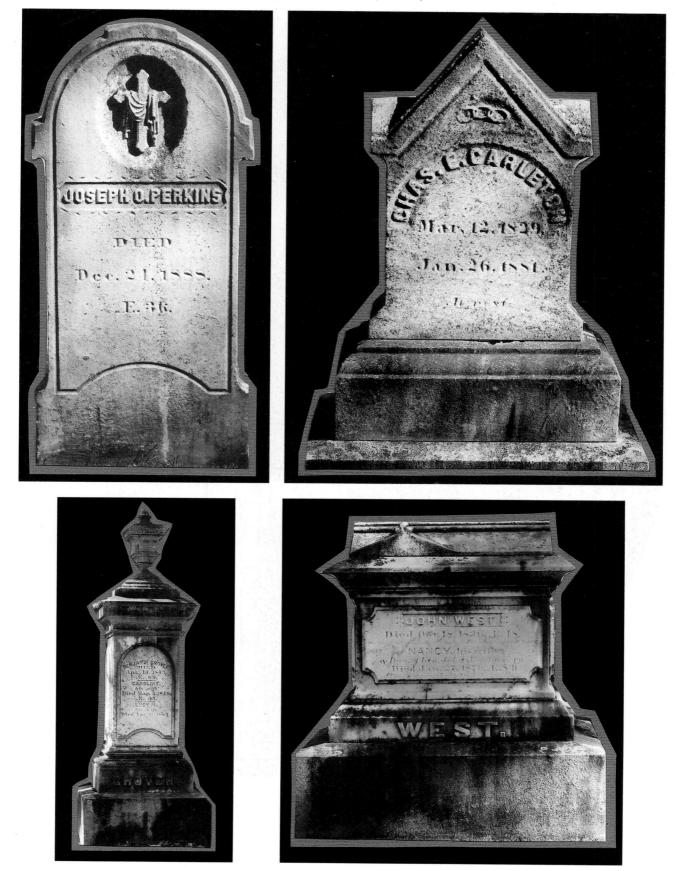

RESOURCES

CAKE AND COOKIE DECORATING

The Baker's Kitchen
TheBakersKitchen.net

Chandlers Cake and Candy Supplies
ChandlersCakeandCandy.com

Chef Tools Network, Inc
ChefTools.com

Fancy Flours
FancyFlours.com

Garnish
ThinkGarnish.com/store

Wilton
Wilton.com

CRAFTS

A.C. Moore Arts & Crafts
ACMoore.com

Anything In Stained Glass
AnythingInStainedGlass.com

Create For Less
CreateForLess.com

Fiskars
Fiskars.com

JoAnn Fabric and Craft Stores
JoAnn.com

June Tailor, Inc.
JuneTailor.com

Michaels Stores
Michaels.com

Molds
Etsy.com/Shop/Molds

ENTERTAINING

Fish's Eddy
FishsEddy.com

Grenon Trading Co.
276 Route 101
Bedford, NH 03110
603/472-3946

OFFICE SUPPLY

The Container Store
ContainerStore.com

Staples
Staples.com

HOME DÉCOR

Bethany Lowe
BethanyLowe.com

Crate & Barrel
CrateAndBarrel.com

Macy's
Macys.com

Matthew Mead Collection
Etsy.com/Shop/MatthewMeadVintage

Pier 1 Imports
Pier1.com

Target
Target.com

TJX Companies
HomeGoods.com

TJMaxx.com

MarshallsOnline.com

West Elm
WestElm.com

WRAPPING PAPERS AND PARTY SUPPLIES

Paper Mart
PaperMart.com

Paper Source
Paper-Source.com

Pearl River, Inc.
PearlRiver.com

PIKKU
PIKKUwares.com

Red River Paper
RedRiverCatalog.com

NATURE CRAFTS SUPPLIES

Attar Herbs and Spices
AttarHerbs.com

Nature's Pressed Flowers
NaturesPressed.com

Seashell World
SeashellWorld.com

TEMPLATES & RECIPES

HolidayWithMatthewMead.com

LET THEM EAT CAKE

There's no unlucky number when cake is involved. Ice and decorate 22 cupcakes or more and arrange in your favorite number pattern to delight your favorite ghouls.